AN EDUCATION OF VALUE

An education of value

The purposes and practices of schools

MARVIN LAZERSON
JUDITH BLOCK McLAUGHLIN
BRUCE McPHERSON
AND
STEPHEN K. BAILEY

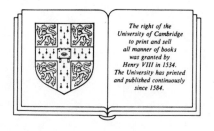

The right of the
University of Cambridge
to print and sell
all manner of books
was granted by
Henry VIII in 1534.
The University has printed
and published continuously
since 1584.

CAMBRIDGE UNIVERSITY PRESS

CAMBRIDGE

LONDON   NEW YORK   NEW ROCHELLE
MELBOURNE   SYDNEY

Published by the Press Syndicate of the University of Cambridge
The Pitt Building, Trumpington Street, Cambridge CB2 1RP
32 East 57th Street, New York, NY 10022, USA
10 Stamford Road, Oakleigh, Melbourne 3166, Australia

First published 1985
Reprinted 1986

Printed in the United States of America

Library of Congress Cataloging in Publication Data
Main entry under title:
An Education of value.
Bibliography: p.
Includes index
1. Education – United States – Aims and objectives.
2. Educational equalization – United States – Addresses,
essays, lectures. 3. Curriculum change – United States –
Addresses, essays, lectures. I. Lazerson, Marvin.
LA217.E36635 1985 370′.973 84-29382
ISBN 0 521 30339 7
ISBN 0 521 31515 8 (pbk.)

TO

Stephen Kemp Bailey
(1916–1982)
and our children,
Jared,
Kerry,
and
Kate

CONTENTS

FOREWORD

This book offers insights into the schools of the United States that are broader and deeper than those in many of the recent reports on education. It brings together a historical sense of how our schools reached their present status, a perspective on the values that undergird educational quality, and a practical concern for how the schools work and what can be done to make them work better.

In dealing with the difficult problem of making useful generalizations about the variety of American schools, this volume is more successful than any we know. It recognizes the diversity, the quality, and the very great achievements of the schools, yet it is uncompromising in calling attention to shallowness within them or in the attitudes of those who plan for their needs. It recognizes significant controversies and deals with them evenhandedly.

An Education of Value is primarily about what goes on inside schools rather than about the activities of state and national governments. When it addresses such national issues as equality of opportunity, it considers their impact on teachers and students. It is full of ideas that can move people who work in schools to action. But these ideas are not presented as a series of steps for improving schools to be used in cookbook fashion. Instead, they are discussed with attention to their origins and values, so that readers are given concepts to inspire action and understanding to ensure that action is based on wisdom.

We undertook to write this brief foreword because both of us were long-time colleagues of Stephen K. Bailey, who originally planned a book about schooling in America with an emphasis on values. We knew him as a thinker and scholar and also as an activist and participant in public affairs, and we admired his capacity to weave these usually separate roles into one life. There are too few like him.

In a sense, the book that has emerged reflects these two faces of Steve Bailey. In doing so, it reaches back to historical and philosophical sources of the American experience, and it combines these with a recognition of what schools are like and what tasks teachers confront. In addressing the large issues of our national experience in education such as the tension between equality and excellence, the book brings qualities of balance, common sense, and understanding based on the historical record that in our view are uniquely valuable to those who must adjust education to the demands of a changing society and economy.

That these qualities pervade the book is partly the result of Stephen Bailey's original conception and his work on the early drafting; they are also present because of the skills and the perceptions of the three co-authors he brought together to work on the manuscript. Marvin Lazerson, Bruce McPherson, and Judith McLaughlin combined scholarly backgrounds in history, the humanities, and education with practical experience to produce a truly interdisciplinary study. They have written a clear and powerful statement about where our schools are, how they got there, and what broad values of the American tradition should be kept in mind by those who would improve them.

Harold Howe II
Francis Keppel
Harvard Graduate School of Education

PREFACE

From September to June each year, some 40 million young people are enrolled in the nation's public schools – kindergarten through twelfth grade. Patently, and in spite of dire claims to the contrary, public schooling is valued. If it were not valued, the nation's citizens would not invest about $127 billion annually in its maintenance. Current expenditures for public schools, even allowing for inflation, have more than tripled in the past twenty-five years. By 1987 they will be at least four times the 1957 expenditures. And, at least in recent years, in most parts of the country these increases have occurred in the face of declining school enrollments.

What is remarkable about the present condition of American public schooling is not the shrillness of public criticism, or the bog of professional despair, but the unfailing continuity of public support. Whatever the doleful criticisms and dire forebodings, public schools remain stable institutions. Viewed historically, they are a remarkable success. Since World War II alone, the percentage of 17-year-olds who graduate from high schools each year has risen from 48% to 75%, from just over 1 million in 1946–7 to over 3 million in the early 1980s – an extraordinary achievement. An increasing number of these youths have come from backgrounds that are educationally and culturally disadvantaged. Schools, to paraphrase Winston Churchill, have brought a growing percentage of the school-age population "under the Constitution."

And yet, paradoxically, the signs of public disaffection with the schools are legion. In 1979, a national sample of 16,000 high school seniors reported that only one-fifth of those questioned were "completely satisfied" with their educational experience. Forty percent were "neutral" to "completely dissatisfied." At the beginning of the 1980s, the Gallup Poll revealed that almost half of the public believed that the schools were doing a poor or only fair job. Only one-third had a great deal of confidence in the people running educational institutions. Recent outbursts of concern from national commissions and studies, and from countless numbers of parents and students, attest both to the sense that something is wrong and to the determination to set the schools right.

To achieve the latter, Americans must take learning and learners seriously. America's schools can be reinvigorated. Young people can learn qualitatively more than they presently do. But these aims will require higher levels of political, moral, and financial commitments to schooling than currently exist. Teaching and learning can be substantially improved. But this will mean valuing teachers more highly and providing the working conditions and incentives that affirm their value.

An Education of Value is designed to stimulate new ways of thinking and talking about schools; it offers an alternative to many educational discussions that too often lead to simplistic solutions to complex problems. Long after the current wave of public interest in the schools has disappeared and the quick fixes have come and gone, the need to continue thinking creatively about schools will persist.

The human dimensions of education complicate the process of improving the schools. Schools are complex institutions. Teaching and learning are exacting activities involving a wide range of emotions and interactions as teachers and students establish who they are and what they want to achieve. The aspirations, fears, frustrations, joys, failures, and accomplishments are intimately bound up in teaching and learning. To treat the problems and the promises of schooling as if these dimensions did not exist, or as if they ought not to exist, devalues what we should cherish. Learning is more than just a cognitive activity; it involves all human experiences. Simplistic notions of learning and teaching limit their possibilities.

Just as the human interactions in school are complex, so too is the institution itself. There is no single "problem" of schooling. The expectations we have for our schools are enormously varied. Yet education is about the things we value. The schools Americans have created are and always have been value laden, and that has aroused inevitable controversy. But we can hardly imagine schools without values, and as long as we differ in values, we will disagree on what we want from schools.

These varied expectations and the multiplicity of values are a strength of our schools. It is a strength we sometimes are too ready to dismiss

xii

in the face of demands that the schools "do it right." We want definite outcomes, clear returns on our investments. So we tell teachers to teach in a certain way or students to learn in a specific manner. But certainty is an illusion. There is no one best way to teach or to learn, no one best form of school organization, or curriculum, or teaching method that applies to us all.

If we can accept the reality that schools are value laden, and that as long as we care about schools they will touch our deepest emotions about ourselves, our children, our past, and our future, we will have come a long way in reshaping our approach to education. We will be able to understand that appeals to or demands for simple solutions, quick fixes, and technological cure-alls are often misguided and counterproductive.

A democracy requires twin goals for education from which there can be no retreat. Schools must be both equal and excellent. Equality in education is predicated on the belief that in a democracy all citizens are entitled to the skills necessary for thoughtful and active citizenship. Excellence in education comes from a commitment to learning, ranging from the basic skills of literacy and problem solving, to creative and critical thinking, to the desire to expand still further one's knowledge and skills. Equality does not require that everyone learn exactly the same things in exactly the same ways. It does require that differences in rates of learning, in interests, and in the purposes of schooling not be used to diminish opportunities to learn or to gain access to knowledge. Differences should not be converted into inequalities.

An Education of Value treats these issues in terms of public schooling. Since its origins in the nineteenth century, the public school has been central to the articulation of America's common purposes. It has embodied the commitment to opportunity and to social improvement, and for that, it has received enormous public support. But it has also been the target of widespread public dissatisfaction. Both the support and the dissatisfaction are measures of the public school's centrality to American life. This book reaffirms that centrality. It expresses the dissatisfactions and hopes in the struggle for schools that are both equal and excellent for all students.

The book is divided into three parts. Part I, "Recurring Priorities, Recurring Tensions," examines the varied historical expectations Americans have held for the schools, how great those expectations have been, and how they have changed over time. The historical analysis presented in Chapter 1 reveals the oversimplifications that can mar our understanding of education. It is designed to distinguish the persistent dilemmas that have faced the schools and to separate them from the ephemeral issues that so often dominate contemporary concerns. The historical record reveals the tension between schools open to all and yet not serving all adequately.

These themes are further developed in the discussion of curriculum reform in Chapter 2. The curriculum is where questions about the transmission of knowledge are centered. What knowledge is most worth having? Should all students learn the same things? Can one curriculum simultaneously enhance equality and excellence? How should we determine what should be taught? Who should make that judgment? These questions have generated some of the most heated controversies in American education. During the 1950s and 1960s, the last great era of curriculum reform, they were manifest in the creation of new curricula in the sciences, mathematics, social studies, English, and foreign languages. The expectations were grandiose, the commitments passionate. The results were often disappointing, in part because the reformers misunderstood the culture of the school. How the curriculum reform movement evolved, and why the disappointments were greater than the satisfactions, is the central focus of the analysis.

Part II, "The Purposes of Schooling," examines equality and excellence. Chapter 3 shows how the shift in education from a nineteenth-century concern with preparing students for moral and political purposes to a twentieth-century concern with preparing them for economic roles sharpened the conflict between equality and educational excellence, at a cost to both. The most obvious manifestation of this has been the tracking system that now afflicts most schools – a way of grouping students that exacerbates their differences in learning styles and capabilities and converts those differences into unequal access to knowledge. The exaggeration of inequality and the lack of excellence serve to undermine one of the most important purposes of schooling: the education of youths for intelligent and active citizenship based on shared skills and knowledge. Excellence for some should not be obtained at the expense of others. The acceptance of inequality corrupts our commitment to learning.

Chapter 4 explores a definition of excellence in learning that sees it as an expansive process involving intellect, emotions, intuition, and will. Learning is objective, passionate, and social. This conception of learning takes us considerably beyond the current view that the schools should first teach basic skills and only later more creative and sophisticated skills. The basic skills of reading, writing, and computing cannot be effectively or meaningfully taught if they are separated from such educational goals as imaginative expression and critical thinking. They ought not to be separated from aesthetics, imagination, and reasoning. Literacy that assumes minimal skill levels is not likely to be achieved, but even more important, it will not motivate students to continue learning. Nor will such low expectations lead to schools in which teachers are passionately committed to teaching.

Part III, "Learning and Teaching," turns to those two issues directly. As a concrete example of the curricular change issues raised in Part II, Chapter 5 examines the promise and the difficulties that educators face in using microcomputers to enhance learning for all students. It addresses questions of access to computers, the use of computers, and how teachers can learn to think imaginatively about their educational uses.

Chapter 6 considers the practice of teaching. The present conditions of teaching militate against new, energetic, creative teaching practices. Teachers are overburdened and underrewarded; they are given few useful opportunities for personal and professional renewal and refreshment. Overwhelmed by the ambiguities and uncertainties inherent in their craft, they know better than anyone else how difficult it is to produce major change in schools. They understand, too, that teaching is a complex and negotiated process; although the teacher teaches something to someone, the learner shapes what and how the something is taught, and in doing so, reshapes the act of teaching itself. Unless teaching is understood as a complicated practice in which the outcomes are always uncertain, and unless what teachers do is taken seriously, there is little chance that learning in the schools will be improved. We need to see teachers as learners and provide them with opportunities to take their own learning seriously.

In Chapter 7 we argue that historical issues in schooling are still active forces, and often powerful determinative factors, in the forging of contemporary policies. The chapter concludes with a reform agenda that begins with the proposition that most reform, to be effective, must begin with empowering teachers, principals, and other educators to improve their own teaching and learning. This agenda emphasizes the desirability of individual schools to have a sense of mission, examines ways in which the quality of teaching and teachers can be improved, and recommends improvements in the selection, education, and perspectives of principals. It urges the formation of coalitions to support public schools and recommends organizational and other changes to enhance the educative power of schools.

Throughout this book, we refer to *American education* and the *schools,* as if there existed a monolith called the *educational system.* But all schools are not the same. Changes will vary with the nature and quality of each school. There are 87,000 public schools in America, located in 16,000 school districts. The problems of an urban secondary school in polyglot Los Angeles are, in many ways, far removed from those of a rural school in South Dakota. Some schools are staffed with well-educated, talented professionals; others are all but overwhelmed by staff mediocrity. These and other variables mean that any generalizations about what exists or what ought to exist in the schools must necessarily be subjected to refinements and qualifications demanded by local specificity. And yet, we can talk about the totality of American education because the cultivation of an informed and expanded intelligence, the enhancement of creative expression and critical thinking, and the development of active and meaningful citizenship cross regional, racial, and class lines.

Many of the recent discussions of education tend to treat the schools in utilitarian terms, arguing that an improved educational program can enhance America's prosperity, increase productivity, and reduce unemployment. We hope that schools will in fact contribute to these ends. One of the functions of this book is to reaffirm the instrumental potential of education. But we also believe that education is more than an instrument. Education is preeminently its own justification, and in the process of becoming educated we become more fully human. From this may flow all kinds of derivative values, but the ultimate value of education is an enlightened mind and the released powers of individuals – alone and together.

ACKNOWLEDGMENTS

An Education of Value came into being through the initiative of Stephen K. Bailey, former Francis Keppel Professor of Policy and Administration at the Harvard Graduate School of Education. Steve Bailey spent most of his professional life engaged in efforts to improve American education. Believing that public education could enhance individual freedom and foster democratic communities, he made what he called "the case for optimism." When he surveyed the educational landscape in the early 1980s, however, he was deeply disturbed by the loss of faith in schooling. This book grew out of his belief in the need to elevate the caliber of the discussion about schools.

As president of the National Academy of Education, Steve Bailey organized a panel of distinguished educators who informed the early stages of this study. Our thanks to José Cardenas, Joseph Featherstone, Patricia Albjerg Graham, Thomas Green, Arthur Jefferson, Diane Ravitch, Joseph Schwab, Lee Shulman, Theodore Sizer, Martin Trow, and David Tyack.

In preparing this work, we met with a number of teachers throughout the country to gain their perspectives on educational issues. The teachers were identified by the National Education Association and the American Federation of Teachers. Background papers were prepared by Gary Engle, James Flood, Al Hurwitz, Brian Larkin, Michael McPherson, and James Rutherford. We wish to thank all of them for their generous help and important insights.

Lord Bullock, past Master of St. Catherine's College of Oxford, and Shepard Stone, Director of the Aspen Institute for Humanistic Studies in Berlin, arranged a seminar for us to present an initial version of the manuscript to a distinguished group of European and American educators, journalists, and policymakers in Berlin. We want to thank James Cooney and Hanna-Beate Schöpp-Schilling of the Institute, and Helmut Becker, Alain Bienaymé, James Coleman,

Acknowledgments

Hermann Granzow, Hanna-Renate Laurien, Sixten Marklund, Stuart Maclure, U. J. Kledzik, Hartmut Rahn, Peter Roeder, Uwe Schlicht, and Helga Thomas.

Many colleagues read and criticized parts of the manuscript: Anthony Bryk, Eleanor Farrar, Barbara Heyns, Ellen Condliffe Lagemann, Magdalene Lampert, and Lauren Young. We are grateful to Gail Keeley and Mary Sullivan for their secretarial assistance and to Leonie Gordon, who typed the bulk of the manuscript.

Our special thanks to Joseph Duffey, Patricia Albjerg Graham, Theodore Sizer, Harold Howe II, and Francis Keppel for advice, criticism, and continuing encouragement. Our deep appreciation to our spouses and friends, Anne Hawley, Ted McLaughlin, Bee Beaudoin, David Cohen, and Ursula Wagener, who shared the struggles and satisfactions with us.

The project was funded by grants from the Lilly Endowment, Inc., and the National Endowment for the Humanities (NEH). We want to thank Laura Bornholdt, Vice President for Education of the Lilly Endowment, and William Bennett, then Chairman of NEH. Armen Tashdinian, Director, Office of Planning and Policy Assessment of NEH, also helped us throughout this project. Joseph Duffey, a past Chairman of NEH, helped initiate the project and was a continuing source of support.

Somewhat different versions of Chapters 2 and 4 appear in *Teachers College Record* and *Daedalus,* respectively. We thank those publications for permission to use the essays in this volume.

On March 27, 1982, with the study in its early stages, Steve Bailey died of cancer. As Steve's co-authors, we undertook to complete the work he had set in motion. *An Education of Value* was inspired by Steve's vision for American education and stands as a memorial to him. Full responsibility for its contents, though, rests solely with us.

M.L.
J.B. McL.
B. McP.
Cambridge, Mass.

PART I
RECURRING PRIORITIES, RECURRING TENSIONS

I

THE EXPECTATIONS OF SCHOOLING

WE have always expected so many contradictory things from our public schools. We have turned to public education to secure a common citizenship and a common morality in a pluralist society, but have often found that this common morality abuses our religious beliefs or ethnic values. We have expected public schools to enhance economic productivity and individual economic opportunity, but have complained that such an emphasis exacerbates individualism and materialism. We have believed that public schools should be cosmopolitan and should share in the nation's goals, but we have also insisted that the educational system be decentralized and that schools be responsive to local values. We have asked public school teachers to assume more tasks and to be responsible professionals, but we underpay them, devalue their work, and blame them for failing to achieve what may be impossible expectations.

Our expectations for education have led us to extend schooling to more and more people for longer periods of time. The commitment to popularization and the expansion of opportunity have crossed social class, racial, and gender lines. Laborers, artisans, farmers, manufacturers, and professionals, whites and nonwhites, immigrants and native-born, women and men have all, at various times, sought to expand schooling for themselves, for their children, and for the children of others.

Yet, the expectations themselves have also been the source of tension and conflict. Sometimes the hopes have been too grandiose, more than should legitimately be expected of any single institution. When the hopes fall short of fulfillment, as they inevitably have, the schools are then promptly condemned for "failing." Sometimes the expectations are contradictory – to eliminate class differences and to reinforce the social class structure, for example – and the result, inevitably, is conflict. Public education is both the source of America's most noble hopes and the repository of its greatest frustrations. Public education expresses our common purposes and our pluralism, our desire for equality and for excellence. Understanding those purposes in common and in conflict, and the ways they have and have not been implemented, is a necessary step in understanding how we can achieve an education of value for all.

EDUCATION: FOR WHOM?

Religion and politics were integral to the origins of public education. In the mid-nineteenth century, public schools had dual and interrelated purposes: to inculcate a sufficient level of Protestantism to assure public and private morality, and to teach a sufficient level of literacy to assure appropriate political choices in a republic.

From the beginning, schools had a special role in preparing the next generation for the responsibilities of citizenship. With large numbers of Americans entitled to a say in governing themselves, some schooling was necessary to ensure appropriate and reasoned choices. Thomas Jefferson captured the essential belief: For the republic to survive, he wrote, the diffusion of "knowledge more generally through the mass of people" was required. This theme was almost universally articulated; a self-governing people needed universal education.[1]

Citizenship was inseparable from religion. Although Americans had rejected an established church, the majority nonetheless expected American society to be religious and Protestant. In relatively homogeneous Protestant communities, the goal of a common Christianity through schooling was easily achieved as communities reached a consensus on such issues as Bible reading, prayers, and holiday observances. In such communities, the district school could also act as the community's major social center. The small white building, a nineteenth-century resident of Prairie View, Kansas, wrote, "was not only the schoolhouse, but the center – educational, social, dramatic, political, and religious – of a pioneer community of the prairie region of the West." Public meetings, spelling bees, political debates, and social gatherings centered on the schoolhouse.[2]

Public schools, however, were never exclusively extensions of homogeneous local communities. The very idea of a *common* school was that it incorporated a varied clientele. In urban areas especially, ethnic and religious heterogeneity and racial and class divisions often made schools the focus of sharp political conflict. In New York City during the 1830s and 1840s, Catholics and Protestants clashed over what constituted an acceptable moral education, and over such questions as whether there should be nonsectarian Bible reading or whether each religious denomination should receive public funds for its own schools. Both sides agreed, however, that the essential purposes of education were moral. Later in the nineteenth century, Catholics of different nationalities created competing parochial schools, as East European Catholics often refused to send their children to the Irish Catholic school or to the local public school. The families believed that schools should defend ethnic cultures; where they did not, parents should send their children elsewhere. Throughout the century, white and black communities contested with one another and argued among themselves over the integration of the schools. In Boston in the 1840s, a coalition of white abolitionists and blacks demanded that black children be allowed to attend integrated schools, were denied their request by the Massachusetts Supreme Court, and then won their cause when the legislature outlawed segregated schools in 1855. In Ohio in the 1850s, state legislation required public financing of black schools, but local hostility from whites was often so great that few black schools were funded.[3]

In most of these conflicts, the contestants agreed on the importance of schooling. They combined to emphasize what schools ought to do. They disagreed on who should go to school and for what purposes. Although parents wanted their children to attend school, they did not expect to abdicate responsibility for what took place there, and many believed that the school should express their own particular values. Time and again, they and their children sought the right to participate in the choice of curriculum, to determine appropriate discipline, and to influence styles of teaching. But parents also felt ambivalent about this right, for they wanted the school to make life for their children a little better than it had been for them, and they were willing to cede power to the professionals who could promise such improvement.

Sometimes the conflicts were over the most basic rights of citizenship and opportunity in a democracy. Perhaps nowhere was this more apparent than in the struggles over the right of freed slaves to attend school. A Mississippi freedman spoke for many blacks: "If I . . . do nothing more while I live, I shall give my children a chance to go to school, for I considers education next best thing to liberty." The conviction that ignorance was its own bondage drew hundreds of thousands to the freedmen's schools. The struggle was difficult and courageous. W. E. B. Du Bois estimated that southern blacks, through voluntary contributions and taxes, paid for their schools and some of the whites' schools, in addition to the voluntary labor needed to organize, build, and maintain their schools.[4]

The hopes of southern blacks were tempered by two fundamental realities, however. Extreme poverty forced many to forgo schooling; next to the economic struggle to survive, any schooling was a luxury. The desire for education was also dangerous. A Virginia black made the point succinctly just after the Civil War: "There are not colored schools down in Surry county; they would kill anyone who would go down there and establish colored schools."[5] Countless blacks, sometimes with white support, struggled against the realities of poverty and danger, for they and their opponents understood that gaining (or withholding) an education was important. On that, most Americans seem to agree.

THE CONDITIONS OF LEARNING

Americans have valued the right to go to school and, as the case of conflict over black schooling suggests, they have recognized the potential of education to disrupt the system of caste. For much of the nineteenth century, they were also fairly certain about what ought to be learned: the community's moral and religious code and basic literary skills in reading, writing, and computation. Most children never went beyond the elementary grades. Teachers presented the daily lesson; students recited passages from textbooks, worked at their desks, or listened to the teacher or to their classmates' recitations.

Teachers presumed that their students would assimilate the material they presented, usually by memorization. An account of an 1892 geography class in Boston is representative:

> Teacher: With how many senses do we study geography?
> Student: With three senses: sight, hearing, and touch.
> The children were now told to turn to the maps of North America in their geographies. . . . When the map had been found each pupil placed his forefinger upon "Cape Farewell," and when the teacher said "Start" the pupils said in concert "Cape Farewell," and then ran their fingers down the map, calling out the names of each cape as it was touched. . . . When the books had been closed, they ran their fingers

down the cover and named from memory the capes in their order from north to south.[6]

The presumption that all students would learn all material did not mean that there were never any distinctions made among pupils. Children were recognized as slow or fast learners, good with the books, or quick with their memories. However, the categories were vague. Establishing different levels of ability with precision was central neither to teaching nor to the curriculum. Because so few children would go on to advanced schooling, determining how much they could learn was of little consequence.

In the twentieth century, the organization of schooling and assumptions about how much schooling was necessary began to change. Shifts in the economy, technological transformations, heightened urban and industrial growth, and the surge of European immigrants intensified the search for institutions that were efficient, orderly, and more predictable. Growing school enrollments, the economic costs of mass education, and the heterogeneity of urban school populations led reformers to reexamine the organization of schooling and the conditions of learning. Age-graded classrooms established a time and place for each child. Centralized and standardized curricula introduced a stepladderlike approach to learning, making it clear when a child was being left behind. With the class expected to do each day's work, and, in so doing, to finish the year's curriculum, daily attendance assumed a new importance. At the same time, mass attendance brought into and kept in the schools youths who previously would have left. The rush to make efficient a bureaucratized, expensive, and mass institution forced to the surface questions about the efficiency of teaching and learning. What were the differences among children? How could they be measured? What kinds of curriculum and teaching were suitable for what kinds of students?

Nowhere were these questions more provocatively posed than in surveys in the first decades of the twentieth century, many directed at how well – or, more accurately, how poorly – children were doing in the schools. The most prominent survey, *Laggards in the Schools* (1908), by Leonard Ayres, concluded that "about one-sixth of all of the children are repeating [the same grade] and we are annually spending about $27,000,000 in their wasteful process of repetition in our cities alone." Ayres and others found that a significant percentage of elementary school children were performing well below

7

what should have been expected of them. Uncertain about why the proportion of repeaters was so high, Ayres was cautious about laying blame, believing that illness, irregular attendance, late age of school entry, lax enforcement, or nonexistent compulsory attendance laws all played a part in contributing to the problem.[7]

Other commentators were less reticent than Ayres in designating the culprits: irrelevant curriculum, poor teaching, and inferior students. The U.S. Senate's Immigration Commission, for example, suggested that low levels of literacy among recent immigrants were due to the "inherent racial tendencies" of each group. The fact that the children of South and East European immigrants were often older than other students in the same grade meant that they were considered "retarded" in the jargon of the day, and thereby reinforced the Immigration Commission's racist assumptions that some nationality groups were less capable of learning than others. In fact, the commission's data did not substantiate its conclusions about the relationship between nationality, race, and education, and certainly not about the capacity to learn. Immigrants were achieving at about the same rates they always had; variables like length of time in the United States explained more about school achievement than did nationality.[8] But the power of the argument that there were sharp, genetically determined limits to learning capacity proved immense, in part because of the growing status of intelligence (IQ) tests.

The debate about IQ tests was intense from the beginning. In France, Alfred Binet had developed the IQ test to identify children in need of special educational treatment. But he was cautious about his measure, writing in 1905, "The scale, properly speaking, does not permit the measure of the intelligence, because intellectual qualities are not superposable, and therefore cannot be measured as linear surfaces are measured." He urged users to remember that IQ was an average of multiple activities, cautioning that the numerical outcome, "if accepted arbitrarily, may give place to illusions." Binet insisted that his test provided no evidence for why children differed in their scores, and he warned against the perversion of IQ into a label that defined and categorized students: "It is really too easy to discover signs of backwardness in an individual when one is forewarned. This would be to operate as the graphologists did who, when Dreyfus was believed to be guilty, discovered in his handwriting signs of a traitor or a spy." Binet's fear, in today's terms, was of using his tests as a self-fulfilling prophecy.[9]

In the United States, Binet's cautions were disregarded and his warnings were systematically rejected. American testers quickly assumed that IQ was a measure of intelligence and should be used to rank children on a scale from supernormal to subnormal. They also believed that IQ tests revealed innate capacities. As Stephen Jay Gould has noted, "American psychologists perverted Binet's intention and invented the hereditarian theory of IQ." They "developed a series of specious arguments confusing cultural differences with innate properties," and they assumed that "inherited IQ scores marked people and groups for an inevitable station in life."[10]

American psychologists and educators used IQ to reinforce tendencies toward group stereotyping about learning and to justify the differentiation of students within schools. Lewis Terman, the country's leading exponent of IQ and the creator of the Stanford-Binet test, outlined the essential argument:

> The intelligence of the average negro is vastly inferior to that of the average white man. The available data indicate that the average mulatto occupies about a mid-position between pure negro and pure white. The intelligence of the American Indian has also been overrated, for mental tests indicate that it is not greatly superior to that of the average negro. Our Mexican population, which is largely of Indian extraction, makes little if any better showing. The immigrants who have recently come to us in such large numbers from Southern and Southeastern Europe are distinctly inferior mentally to the Nordic and Alpine strains we have received from Scandinavia, Germany, Great Britain, and France.[11]

In practice, of course, schools did not treat IQ simply as a reflection of a group's capacity to learn. Most teachers evaluated their students on the basis of daily classroom performance. Nor were all who believed in the use of IQ tests racists. Many, like the sociologist and educator Horace Mann Bond, thought that IQ tests could be used to explore learning differences and to develop curriculum. But the hope that intelligence tests would be used primarily to enhance learning was undermined by the assumption that IQ measured inherent capacities. Try as some testers might to show that a battery of tests could be used to measure capacity (IQ) and levels of knowledge (achievement tests), which could then be used to determine which children needed more educational practice and exposure, the frequent practical effect of the tests was to lock youths into special curricula – special education classes, vocational programs, college-bound courses. The idea that science could be used to evaluate learning and to extend equality of opportunity gave way before the notion that scientific measurement would highlight the limits of learning.

The new emphasis on measuring capabilities that emerged in the 1920s propelled the issue of ability grouping to the fore. The issue was not entirely new. Nineteenth-century educational reformers had believed that students would learn more if they were grouped into grades rather than simply gathered together, as they were, in one-room schoolhouses. As a major innovation, the Quincy School, which opened in Boston in 1848, contained twelve classrooms, each with a separate teacher teaching a separate grade. The students were divided by proficiency, and as Boston's future superintendent of schools wrote, "all in the same class attend to precisely the same branches of study." By 1870, most large American cities had established graded schools based primarily on the age of the student. The new system allowed for the "division of labor in educational matters." "The teacher's time and talents being concentrated upon certain work, it becomes easier by repetition, and therefore, is likely to be performed more efficiently." With graded schools came pressure for uniform courses of study, standardized examinations, specialized teacher training, methods of evaluating teaching, timetables, and a host of other schoolwide and system-wide attributes.

The post–World War I debate over the relationship between ability grouping and learning was thus continuous with earlier concerns. But in the 1920s and 1930s, it was fueled by the coincidence of three conditions. First, the surge of interest in ability grouping was based upon a mass elementary and secondary educational system. Especially as students continued through high school, the issue of how to distinguish among them became prominent. Second, ability grouping drew upon the assumption that there ought to be a close relationship between what one learned in school and what one needed for occupational success outside of school. The curriculum ought to be varied because economic roles varied. And third, grouping depended upon the new instruments for measuring ability.

The impact of measurement was profound; its scientific imprimatur fulfilled the powerful need to justify educational reform on scientific grounds. A New York City superintendent of schools articulated in 1922 what was rapidly becoming orthodoxy among American educators: "We stand on the threshold of a new era in which we will increasingly group our pupils on the basis of both intelligence and accomplishment quotients and of necessity, provide differentiated curricula, varied modes of instruction, and flexible promotion to meet the crying needs of our children."[12]

During the 1920s, grouping by ability grew by leaps and bounds. In 1926, the U.S. Bureau of Education reported that thirty-seven out of forty cities with populations of over 100,000 used ability grouping in some or all elementary grades, and a slightly lower percentage did so in junior and senior high schools. By 1930, ability grouping was being hailed as a major advance in school organization and teaching.[13]

The justifications for grouping varied, but they tended to fall into two categories: administrative and pedagogical efficiency and adherence to democratic precepts. Ability grouping would allow schools and teachers to develop differentiated curricula and pedagogical styles appropriate to students' learning capacities. It would enhance learning for the slow as well as the fast learner. But because separating students, especially young ones, by capability seemed to undermine the widespread belief that education should be available to all, with all students learning roughly the same things in roughly the same ways, ability grouping required a more sweeping justification than administrative and pedagogical efficiency. An alternative philosophy of democratic education was necessary: Individuals had different capacities and interests, and a truly democratic education would accede to those differences by providing educational experiences congruent with them. A democratic education was one in which students learned different things in different ways. The conditions of learning were best provided in schools that offered a varied curriculum and varied teaching styles.

In practice, school systems blended uniformity and variety. Public elementary schools were, on the whole, common in the sense that they were neighborhood schools; all who chose to could attend. The most important forms of segregation were racial and class. The use of district boundaries to enforce racial segregation and the costs of residential housing meant that neighborhood schools often reflected class and racial divisions. Within elementary classrooms, excessive and highly formalized differentiation by ability groups was limited. Parents and many educators resisted tracking of young children. An East European immigrant mother put the case as succinctly as possible: "You can't put my Tony in the dumbbell school."[14]

By the 1930s, the question of who would learn how much with

whom was answered with a mixture of optimism and pessimism about how much could be learned by all, and of integration and segregation in the grouping of students. The belief that more and more schooling was good for the individual and for society was paralleled by a science that stressed the limits of learning capability. Universal schooling meant that every child was expected to attend school, but measurements of capability meant that within the universal system, students were differentiated by how much – or, actually, how little – they were expected to learn.

As the length of schooling was extended for more and more students, the expectations that some could learn only a little and others a lot, and that students also ought to learn different things, were accentuated. The higher one went up the academic ladder, the more grouping occurred, with different groups learning different things. The junior high school was predicated, in part, on the desire to differentiate youths on the basis of abilities and likely occupational roles. In senior high schools, students were grouped into occupational categories: college bound, vocational/industrial (boys), vocational/clerical (girls), and a catchall category often called *general*. As was true of ability grouping, the categories were defined largely by class, race, and gender. For example, boys were overwhelmingly more likely to be placed in special education and low-ability groups than were girls, reflecting the extent to which ability grouping was dependent on behavioral attributes. The irony was that the public school was simultaneously a place where students learned in common and a place where they were sharply differentiated.

AMBIVALENT SUPPORT

As a public institution, the school was supposed to serve parental as well as community desires. The school was a voluntary institution, and parents believed that it should conform to their values. Calling the teacher to task was not uncommon. Nineteenth-century parents were quick to exercise that dearly held prerogative, as in the case of one parent who wrote to a teacher:

Sir:

I am very sorry to informe that in my opinion you have Shoed to me that you are unfit to keep a School, if you hit my boy in the face accidentley that will be different but if on purpose Sir you are unfit for the Business.[15]

The status of teachers reflected this public accountability. Mid-nineteenth-century teachers lacked modern bureaucratic buffers and the distancing mechanisms of professionalism. The quality of their teaching was regularly judged in public spelling bees, declamations, and examinations. Their personal behavior and morals were closely scrutinized, their pay was poor, and annual appointments meant insecurity from year to year. Even those who were considered administrators were scrutinized in their personal as well as professional behavior. To survive, they had to be "one of the boys."

The bureaucratization of school systems after the late nineteenth century freed educators from many direct forms of parental and community intervention. Much did remain continuous: the expectation of appropriate moral behavior, doubts about legitimate professional autonomy, the need for an administrator to be an "old boy," and the intervention of parents into the teaching process when they believed their values were being violated. Nonetheless, twentieth-century educators made the case that their competence and expertise entitled them to independence and public support.

Tensions between schools and communities remained, then as now, over the school's role in presenting children with alternatives to parental and community values, between a family's economic needs and the possible economic benefits of extending schooling, and over the dilemmas of professionalism in a public institution.

A continuing source of concern was what schools should teach. Parents often wanted teachers to reinforce their own values and their parental authority, while simultaneously expecting teachers to prepare their children for the larger opportunities of American life – to identify themselves as Americans if they were immigrants, to identify with a world beyond the household, and, increasingly in the twentieth century, to gain the social and technical skills for economic success. Many teachers hoped that their labors would extend the child's horizons beyond the parochialism of the community. Hamlin Garland recalled how effectively the McGuffey Readers had fulfilled that expectation in nineteenth-century Iowa: "I wish to acknowledge my deep obligation to Professor McGuffey, whoever he may have been, for the dignity and literary grace of his selections. From the pages of his readers I learned to know and love the poems of Scott, Byron, Southey, Wordsworth and a long line of the English masters."[16] Although other students viewed their lessons less favorably, and certainly many teachers were ignorant and fearful of the world beyond their communities, still the textbooks used in schools often revealed to the student a world beyond the boundaries of New York's East Side, the Kansas town, or the Mississippi cotton plantation.

Educators thus engaged in frequent give-and-take with parents, who were themselves ambivalent about their aspirations for their children.[17] The process led to tensions over how far beyond community and parental values the schools should go. Not surprisingly, many of the tensions involved religious values. From the early nineteenth century to the present, "school wars" have regularly erupted over appropriate forms of religious instruction, over school prayers, over whether the Bible was sectarian, and over "godless" secularism in textbooks. The establishment and growth of Protestant, Catholic, and Jewish alternatives to the public schools, and the controversies from the early twentieth century on over the relationship of evolution to religion – highly publicized in events like the Scopes trial during the 1920s and the current controversies over creationism versus Darwinism – reveal the uneasy dilemma of trying to teach a larger audience than the local community of particular families while still accommodating the latter.

Similar tensions have affected curriculum reforms. During the 1960s, the nationally and university-based *Man: A Course of Study (MACOS)* social studies curriculum unit was widely acclaimed for applying new scientific knowledge on what human beings and other animals had in common and was heatedly attacked for violating religious precepts on the distinctions between humans and animals. MACOS had sources of funding outside local school districts and attracted attention at the federal level, but the decentralized character of American education meant that the battles over its use were first waged in local communities. These battles often pitted those pleased with the curriculum's innovativeness and cosmopolitan approach against those appalled at its violation of their deeply held religious beliefs. Teachers were invariably caught in the middle, many wanting a promising curricular innovation, uncertain about how to use it, and unhappy at the conflict its use engendered.

To be sure, the degree of conflict over religion and curriculum can be overdrawn. Many teachers have been products of the communities they taught in, and their values have often paralleled those of their students' parents. Most of what happens in school has gone unnoticed. But the school has always had obligations beyond the local community: The responsibility of schooling to extend students' horizons and the possibility that school-learned literacy might be liberating have made even the most locally tied teacher an agent of change.

For many parents and their children, commitment to schooling has also been shaped by the family's economic needs. In nineteenth-century rural America, schooling accommodated the seasonal rhythms of agricultural production. Older youths attended school during the winter and left as soon as their labor was required for farm and household economies. In urban areas, similarly, nineteenth-century youths moved in and out of schools according to the exigencies of the labor market. Recognizing these situations, rural and urban school reformers concentrated their attention on separating education from employment. School was something one attended, they argued, no matter what work was available or what a family's economic situation was. But the efforts to keep young people in school – by extending the age of compulsion and enforcing compulsory statutes – often conflicted with the desires of parents and youths. Working-class families in particular would trade off potential future returns from schooling for more immediate economic returns. In an economically insecure world, the extra income might be used to buy a house, which seemed a surer way to gain security than the less certain possibility that a few more years in school would lead to greater income for the family.[18]

The growing professionalization of public education provoked further tension between the school and parents. Based on notions of expertise and benevolence – that educators were both competent and acted in the best interests of the child – professionalization enhanced educators' freedom to choose the appropriate curriculum and pedagogy, to evaluate students, and to determine the best school program. But because school financing and governance were public, teachers needed as much community support as possible. Educators were thus forced into an ambivalent relationship with parents: At the same time as they called for parental involvement, they decried parental interference. For parents, this dilemma took a different shape. In school committee elections, school bond votes, and informal and formal consultations, parents had a voice in educational decision making. Yet they were told that educators had the competence to make the right decisions for their children and that educators ought to be as free as possible to make those decisions.[19]

As schools became the central agency in moving children from the family to the adult world, parents looked to them with both optimism and trepidation. School attendance became required – in a formal legislative sense and as a necessary step toward selected occupations – but the returns were never guaranteed. Schools tended toward a cosmopolitanism about which many parents were uncertain. Educators simultaneously demanded autonomy and public support. The ambivalence that resulted became – and remains – the basis of both the approval and the frustration with which Americans view their schools.

THE COMPREHENSIVE CURRICULUM

One source of popularity was the expectation that the schools would serve useful economic and social functions. Throughout the nineteenth century, educators regularly added new courses to the curriculum on the basis of their utility, a process that was accelerated after 1900. For secondary education, the evolution of the arguments supporting the increased variety of courses can be seen in the publication of two major reports on American secondary education: the report of the National Education Association (NEA) Committee of Ten in 1893 and the NEA Commission on the Reorganization of Secondary Education's *Cardinal Principles of Secondary Education* in 1918.

Headed by Harvard's President Charles William Eliot, the Committee of Ten was appointed to introduce greater rationality and uniformity into secondary education. Eliot was highly critical of the educational offerings of schools. Pupils, he complained, "may now go through a secondary school course of a very feeble and scrappy nature – studying a little of many subjects and not much of any one, getting, perhaps, a little information in a variety of fields, but nothing which can be called a thorough training." The committee argued that although students should continue to choose among different courses of study – accepting the reality that was already occurring – every course ought to have the same ends: "training the powers of observation, memory, expression, and reasoning," and teachers had to be more effectively trained to those ends.[20]

Twenty-five years later, with the high school on its way to becoming a universal institution, the Commission on the Reorganization of Secondary Education issued perhaps the most famous pronouncement on American high schools (prior to that of James B. Conant), pushing the idea of a diversified curriculum and student choice considerably beyond that advocated by the Committee of Ten: "Secondary education should be determined by the needs of the society to be served, the character of the individuals to be educated, and the knowledge of educational theory and practice available. These factors are by no means static." The phrases were trite, but their meaning became clear as the report elaborated on the purposes of secondary schooling.

The commission urged that the curriculum reflect the variations of social life and of students, and that courses be considered, not as teaching "general discipline," but as training for specific relevance and practical outcomes. The curriculum should be inclusive. Social studies should offer "such topics as community health, housing and homes, public recreation, good roads, community education, poverty and the care of the poor, crime and reform, family income saving bonds and life insurance, human rights versus property rights, impulsive action of mobs, the selfish conservatism of tradition, and public utilities."[21]

The positions articulated by the 1918 commission soon became the practice of American education. Sociologists Helen and Robert Lynd recorded what they found in Muncie, Indiana, during the mid-1920s. A freshman could choose among 12 different programs and, over four years, from 102 separate courses. This was something new, the Lynds reported. Thirty years earlier, students could choose between only two programs, Latin and English, and from a total of twenty separate courses.[22]

By the post–World War II period, educators assumed that an adequate secondary curriculum required an extensive number of courses. James B. Conant summarized the common wisdom in 1959 when he called for the consolidation of high schools, which were "too small to allow a diversified curriculum except at exorbitant expense. The prevalence of such high schools – those with graduating classes of less than one hundred students – constitutes one of the serious obstacles to good secondary education throughout most of the United States."[23]

In the 1950s, the concern with comprehensiveness was paralleled by appeals for academic rigor. The Cold War and the widespread talk of a "knowledge explosion" led to a host of curriculum innovations to upgrade standards; the new physics and new mathematics of the late 1950s were soon followed by major reform efforts in the other sciences, social studies, languages, and English.

The attempt to introduce greater academic rigor into the comprehensive curriculum – an issue we pursue more fully in Chapter 2 – was fraught with difficulties. Greater academic commitment competed with the social and athletic activities that students found more attractive. Tracked programs placed a ceiling on expectations about how much and what students could learn. By the early 1960s, a common view of the curriculum – which only later would become disturbing – was established: The more courses a school had, the better the curriculum. The corollary was even more disturbing: Academic excellence was not crucial to school learning.

LEARNING TO EARN

Between the ages of seven and twelve, most children in nineteenth-century America were enrolled in schools. After age twelve, however, both enrollment and attendance declined sharply. Working-class and poor youths left school early, probably whenever they could find employment – for boys most often as unskilled laborers, for girls as domestic servants or factory workers. The work was irregular and insecure, and young people moved frequently among jobs, unemployment, and schooling. Because the schools were not directly linked to job skills or did not necessarily provide access to most occupations, even the children of middle-class and professional parents did not remain enrolled for long.[24]

Some schooling in the nineteenth century did have economic relevance. In the 1840s, Horace Mann cited its contributions to economic success to justify public education: Educated individuals were more productive than the uneducated, and therefore their economic worth was greater. High school completion probably enhanced educational opportunities. Popular culture occasionally suggested that education was important to success. In Horatio Alger's *Ragged Dick,* for example, the main protagonist, Dick Hunter, asks his homeless but educated friend Fosdick to share his living quarters:

> I'll make a bargain with you. I can't read much more'n a pig; and my writin' looks like hen's tracks. I don't want to grow up known' no more'n a four-year-old boy. If you'll teach me readin' and writin' evenin's, you shall sleep in my room every night.

18

Not long afterward, Fosdick gets a job and expresses disappointment that Dick does not yet have one. Dick's response affirms his belief in education as an avenue of success: "I don't know enough yet. Wait till I've gradooated."[25]

Still, the expectation that schooling translated into vocational success was a minor theme in the nineteenth century. The older values of perseverance and moral rectitude, rather than the newer value of formal schooling, were presumed to lead to economic mobility. And these older values could often be learned better outside of school. Most occupations did not, in fact, require much literacy. Paradoxically, too much schooling was often considered detrimental to an individual's economic success.

Exactly when schooling became important to occupational success is unclear. What is certain is that by the 1930s, the relationship between youth, work, and schooling had changed as more and more teenagers delayed entry into the labor market and stayed in school. The gross statistics are striking. The percentage of 14 to 18-year-old males at work dropped from 43% in 1900 to 12% by 1930. For females, the decline was from 18% to 5%. Simultaneously, high school enrollment of 14 to 17-year-olds between 1900 and 1930 climbed from almost 8% to over 44%. Clearly, not all youths left the labor market and went to school. With some exceptions, school attendance was more extensive in the cities than in rural and agricultural areas; more extensive for the children of professionals than for those of the working class; more for Jews than for southern Italians; more for whites than for nonwhites; and more likely when labor market conditions were bad. But the trend was clear and powerful: Regional, ethnic, racial, gender, and class differences in length of school attendance narrowed considerably as adolescents withdrew from full-time employment and stayed in school.[26]

Young people deferred entry into the labor market and stayed in school longer for a variety of reasons. More rigorous enforcement of child labor and compulsory attendance laws undoubtedly played some role in making it more difficult for young teenagers to find work. Public concern about the immorality and potential delinquency of youths on the street led to increased pressures to keep them in school. Adolescence was considered a time of preparation for adult responsibilities; schooling was the logical place to keep teenagers sheltered and removed from the adult world. Higher standards of living allowed families to keep their children in school longer. Changes in the schools

themselves – the introduction of progressive pedagogy and modifi-
cations in the curriculum, especially vocational education – probably
made education interesting enough so that those on the borderline
opted to stay in school. There may also have been a kind of snow-
balling effect, apparent by the 1920s, with youths staying in school
in part because their friends were there and in part because the extra
curriculum of athletics, newspapers, and social life made school an
appealing place.

Perceived and actual changes in labor markets also kept adolescents in school longer. In the belief that staying longer in school
improved economic opportunities, employers began to treat more
schooling as a prerequisite for jobs. Personnel officers of large cor-
porations began to use length of schooling as a criterion for hiring.
Many of the skills required to get office jobs – literacy, computation,
bookkeeping, and accounting, as well as the behavioral norms congruent with office and managerial positions – were effectively taught
in school. New office positions were highly stratified by gender: Sec-
retaries, clerks, and bookkeepers were women and placed in low-
paid positions, whereas managers and accountants were men, with
higher pay and status. The increasing status of professional occupations provided a potent symbol of the social status and economic
power that could be gained through educational achievement.

Increasingly, the arguments given for staying in school pointed to
the potential vocational benefits of education. In 1917, the U.S. Bureau
of Education published "The Money Value of Education," an attempt
to estimate the economic returns for each year spent in school. This
theme has remained central to evaluations of educational worth ever
since. Reformers proclaimed that "learning to earn" should be the
central theme of secondary schooling. In the mid-1920s, the president of the Muncie, Indiana, school board was even more explicit:
"For a long time all boys were trained to be President. Then for a
while we trained them all to be professional men. Now we are training boys to get jobs." The schools of Muncie took the task seriously:
Vocational education courses were a central feature of the high school,
and parents agreed that the primary reason for their children to attend
school was to get ahead. Overwhelmingly, in the decades after 1920,
youths justified staying in school on the ground that it would pay
off.[27]

Even with equal schooling, however, the payoffs were not always the same. Discriminatory labor markets limited the advantages of schooling for women and minorities. Early in the twentieth century, William L. Bulkley, New York City's only black school principal, made the point simply by asking rhetorically how he could persuade a black youth to stay in school when the boy "must face the bald fact that he must enter business as a boy and wind up as a boy"[28]

The public perception that the most important role of schooling was preparation for economic roles solidified. Americans continued to talk about the common values and the moral and political aims of schooling in a democracy, but they almost invariably subordinated those values to the expectation that schools should fit youths for the competitive economic race ahead. Adam Smith might have been pleased: Schools functioned best by enhancing the capacity for individual economic success. By the early 1950s, vocational goals had become the dominant justification for public schooling. School attendance meant economic returns. During the 1950s and 1960s, that assumption was justified often enough to take on the attributes of a self-fulfilling prophecy. So strong was this belief that in later years, when the economic returns of schooling became less certain, the schools were judged to be failing.

LESSONS OF THE PAST

We invariably refer to the past to legitimate our beliefs and policies, but we also treat issues as if they had never appeared before. Yet the past lives with us, not just in the sense that our contemporary institutions are its products, but because our system of values is itself historically rooted. What we believe – our ideals, as well as the contradictions implicit in them – are part of our cultural heritage.

America's commitment to schooling is part of that heritage. Popular schooling, initially tied to religion and then to citizenship, existed in the nineteenth century, as Lawrence Cremin notes, "for the purpose of conveying literacy along with a certain common core of knowledge, morality, and patriotism."[29] Over time, the definitions of those terms changed. Literacy developed beyond signing one's name to include reading, writing, and the comprehension of ideas. The common core of necessary knowledge expanded and became fragmented. Morality's ties to religion weakened and became more relative. Patriotism incorporated critical views of one's country and its institutions. Expectations for education expanded to include equalized opportunity and enhanced access to status, wealth, and security.

Since World War II, the expectations of schooling have expanded vigorously. In the last three decades, Americans have engaged in unprecedented efforts to make public schools the central agency of opportunity and equality, of social reform, and of economic productivity and individual gain. Education has expanded from state and local jurisdictions to become part of national politics. Schools have been an issue in every presidential campaign since 1956. Even a partial listing of educational issues recalls some of the most fundamental concerns of postwar America: *Brown* v. *Board of Education,* student demonstrations, the Great Society's Elementary and Secondary Education Act of 1965, Head Start, bilingual education, the education of the handicapped and mainstreaming, desegregation and busing, affirmative action, Scholastic Aptitude Test (SAT) examinations, access to higher education and education for excellence.[30]

Heightened expectations have meant more political and intensified conflicts over schooling than ever before. At times, as Americans have contested the purposes and conditions of schooling, the strains have seemed likely to tear the social fabric. The failures of reform have seemed more dramatic because the hopes have been so high. It is a measure of the importance of schools to our culture that we argue so heatedly about them.

2

NEW CURRICULUM, OLD ISSUES

AMERICANS are both historically oriented and ahistorical. Nowhere is this more apparent than in debates over school curriculum. We lament low academic standards in the schools, call for a return to a lost rigor, and insist on going back to basics. Yet, even as we hold up the past as a standard, we lack understanding of what actually happened in the past. State departments of education rewrite curriculum guides in attempts to strengthen the commitment to learning. School districts trim their curricular offerings and stiffen graduation requirements. In the U.S. Congress and state legislatures, laws are passed to improve science, mathematics, technology, and foreign language instruction. And teachers are being warned to take the academic content of their work more seriously.

As serious as the criticisms are, there is nevertheless a *déja vu* quality to these concerns. They are reminiscent of criticisms raised some twenty-five to thirty years ago. The 1950s and 1960s were the most intense period of curricular reform in American educational history, when the curricula of virtually every academic discipline were under examination. "New mathematics" was substituted for the "old" arithmetic; new physics, chemistry, and biology captured science education; "new social studies" and transformational grammar competed with the familiar history, civics, and grammar courses. The curriculum reformers were determined to change the course offerings of an educational system they believed to be uninspiring, unintellectual, and insufficiently challenging for its most gifted students. At no other time in the nation's history were so many eminent university scholars involved in designing school curricula with so much money available for their efforts.

The educational reformers did not realize their dreams. As they attempted to implement their ideas, they found the task more difficult than they had foreseen. The reformers encountered a host of conflicts in local communities, in the schools, in the academic community, and in their own thinking about education. What seemed clear – the pursuit of academic excellence – became less certain in the shifting sands of implementation and ideological assumptions.

The rhetoric of these earlier curriculum reform efforts was impelled by the perceived need to compete with the Soviets in space and to triumph in the Cold War. Today's rhetoric is markedly similar, with the Japanese economy having been added to the threat. But the earlier reform period differed from that of today in its optimism. Reformers were confident that their new programs would substantially change the content of schooling and that the American educational system would triumph. Jerome Bruner captured the optimistic mood when he wrote in 1960 that "something new was stirring in the land." Distinguished mathematicians at the University of Colorado, the University of Illinois, and Stanford University were writing new textbooks for schools and teaching young children fundamental mathematical concepts; "first-class biologists" in Kansas City were producing films for school biology courses; Massachusetts Institute of Technology (MIT) scientists were preparing an "ideal" physics course for high school students; and chemists in Portland, Oregon were drafting a new chemistry program. In the social sciences, a movement to transform the curriculum was beginning. "Educators and psychologists," Bruner concluded, "were examining anew the nature of teaching methods and curricula and were becoming increasingly ready to examine fresh approaches." Their hope was for nothing less than a revolution in the nature of students' encounters with academic subjects as they modernized course content, introduced new teaching materials, and conveyed to students the excitement of scientific and intellectual inquiry.[1]

What occurred during this period of intense reform efforts is important to understand because it alerts us to be wary of easy rhetoric and simple panaceas. At a time when almost everyone is for higher academic standards and excellence in curriculum, it is imperative to reflect on the complexities and difficulties of educational change. As we debate what constitutes a valued school program, we need to keep the lessons of past curriculum reform efforts clearly in mind. To point to some of these lessons, we examine two prominent efforts to reform the curriculum in the 1950s and 1960s: the new mathematics and the new social studies. These case studies show the high aspirations with which the curriculum reform began and the extensive work that went into the planning, preparation, pilot testing, and evaluation of materials. They reveal why the curriculum reform movement that began with such promise was a disappointment. And they suggest how today's efforts can profit from the lessons of the past.[2]

SCHOOL MATHEMATICS STUDY GROUP (SMSG)

The story of the School Mathematics Study Group (SMSG) begins with two meetings in February 1958. At the first meeting, the Chicago Conference on Research Potential and Training, research mathematicians expressed concern over the low numbers and poor preparation of students electing their field of study. Convinced that the mathematics profession should direct attention to school mathematics programs, the Chicago Conference participants passed a resolution calling for the president of the American Mathematical Society to appoint a committee "to seek funds from suitable sources and proceed toward a solution of the problem" of school mathematics instruction.[3]

Participants in a second meeting, the Mathematics Meeting of the National Science Foundation, held in Cambridge, Massachusetts, exactly one week later, seconded the Chicago Conference resolution. Their meeting had been held at MIT so that the participants could meet with MIT faculty who were involved in the development of a new high school physics curriculum. The mathematicians were impressed with the content and experiential approach of the new physics materials. They wanted to see similar curriculum reform in mathematics, and they recommended that the president of the American Mathematical Society immediately appoint a planning committee to organize a curriculum reform effort for mathematics.

The interest expressed by the mathematicians was not surprising. Mathematics instruction had been a focus of curriculum reform efforts since the early 1950s. The University of Illinois Committee on School Mathematics (UICSM), the first major national curriculum project, was a model for other projects, with its emphasis on the role of university-based researchers and on "learning through discovery" teaching methods. In 1955 the College Entrance Examination Board had appointed a commission "to review the existing secondary school mathematics curriculum, and to make recommendations for its modernization, modification, and improvement," with special attention addressed to the "college capable student."[4] Two years later, mathematicians at the University of Maryland established the University of Maryland Mathematics Project, bringing together university mathematicians and school teachers to prepare experimental mathematics courses for grades seven and eight.

Although American Mathematical Society President Richard Brauer took seriously the two conference recommendations, he nevertheless proceeded cautiously. The American Mathematical Society, the senior and most prestigious mathematics association in the country, had long been removed from considerations of school curriculum. Only after Brauer had secured the support of the society's executive committee did he name eight university mathematicians to a new committee and asked Edward G. Begle of Yale University to serve as project director. Backing by the American Mathematical Society gave the curriculum reform project prominence and credibility. Now it was respectable, even admirable, for senior mathematicians to devote time to the development of school curriculum.

The new committee, the School Mathematics Study Group, invited forty-five mathematics teachers and researchers to Yale University for a five-week summer program in 1958. Twenty-one of the participants were high school teachers and curriculum supervisors; twenty-one were college and university professors; and three participants represented the Rand Corporation, Bell Laboratories, and the American Association for the Advancement of Sciences. The teachers and curriculum supervisors came from many of the nation's most respected high schools, including the Bronx High School of Science, Phillips Academy, New Trier Township High School, Newton High School, and University High School of the University of Chicago. The participants included authorities in mathematics education, authors of popular textbooks, and officials of local, state, and national professional organizations. For the high school and college mathematics teachers, writing school curriculum together was a new experience.

Their assignment was difficult: In five weeks, the forty-five mathematicians were expected to reach a common definition of a mathematics program and to draft detailed outlines of mathematics texts for that program. These outlines had to be prepared in sufficient detail so that they could be field tested in classrooms during the coming school year and revised and expanded into full texts the following summer. Rather than tackling the entire span of schooling, the SMSG Advisory Board asked the summer writers to develop curriculum for "college-capable" students in grades seven through twelve, that is, those students who were believed most likely to pursue careers requiring training in mathematics.

The participants agreed that the mathematics curriculum in schools needed change. Whereas research mathematics had changed in the previous decade, school mathematics had remained the same. The mathematicians wanted the school curriculum to stress basic concepts rather than the current emphasis on computational skills. They believed that students should develop an understanding of the logic and structure of mathematics and that they should learn mathematical vocabulary.

The participants organized themselves into work teams broken down by school year (seven and eight, nine, ten, eleven, twelve), with each team carefully arranged to include an equal number of secondary school teachers and college professors. The composition of these groups reflected the SMSG staff's commitment to ensuring that the perspectives and expertise of both teachers and professors were involved in curriculum development. After these groups were formed, each team had to wrestle with difficult questions of scope, approach, goals, content, emphasis, level of difficulty, and presentation of course materials.

In thinking through the instructional issues, not all teams started from scratch. The two mathematics curriculum projects that preceded SMSG – the University of Illinois Committee on School Mathematics and the University of Maryland Mathematics Project – were available to the SMSG writers, as were copies of the College Entrance Examination Board's Commission on Mathematics' preliminary report. As the teams produced new curriculum outlines, their peers reviewed them. Issues were discussed and debated, drafts closely scrutinized. No draft was considered final until it had been edited many times. After five weeks of intense work, the job was complete. Curriculum outlines were ready for field testing.

The curriculum outlines were distributed to teachers in the fall of 1958 from "centers" throughout the country. Each center was staffed with a chairman who selected local teachers to field-test the units and a consultant who assisted teachers with instructional problems. Because the consultants were college mathematicians, all centers were located near a college or university. The school year began with an orientation program for participating teachers designed to familiarize them with SMSG materials and to stimulate their excitement and enthusiasm for the curriculum reform movement.

Over the course of the 1958–59 school year, the SMSG staff grew in size as their work expanded in scope. Additional writers were selected to continue writing the text outlines and to prepare monographs to supplement these texts. A panel on in-service training was assigned responsibility for developing teacher-education materials. To spread the word about SMSG, a newsletter was published and SMSG project director Ed Begle spoke about the project at mathematics meetings across the country.

In the summer of 1959, 101 mathematics teachers and researchers took part in SMSG's second summer writing session. As in the previous summer, the writers faced tight publication deadlines: In less than six weeks, they had to produce a completed secondary school textbook series; in two weeks, they had to complete one-third of this series so that it could be printed for classroom use in September. By the end of the second summer session, the SMSG writers had published textbooks and accompanying teacher commentaries for grades seven through twelve. Their success in meeting their production deadlines inspired the SMSG Advisory Board to cast its net wider, and a third grant from the National Science Foundation (NSF) (bringing the total the SMSG had received from the agency to over $4,000,000) made further activities possible. The original SMSG textbook series was directed to secondary school students in the top third of their class in mathematics ability. Now the focus would include curriculum for non-college-bound secondary school students (students in the 25% to 75% range of mathematical ability) and materials for elementary students in grades four through six.

Eighty-seven research mathematicians and mathematics educators participated in SMSG's third writing session in the summer of 1960. They polished the college-capable textbook series, developed outlines for a new elementary school series, and revised the college-capable series for use by "students with undeveloped mathematical talent," the label given to the non-college-bound students in the 25% to 75% ability range. When the summer ended, they had completed the entire series of textbooks for college-capable students and had created outlines for the additional instructional materials.

By the 1960–1 school year, it seemed to many that mathematics education was on the verge of a revolution. Over 130,000 new text-books for college-capable students were in classrooms; an additional 15,000 curriculum outlines were being field tested. High-powered academic mathematicians and school mathematics teachers had col-laborated over the previous four years with a remarkable degree of enthusiasm, commitment, and success. Together, they had intro-duced probably the most innovative and challenging mathematics curriculum materials ever produced for American school children. Even the younger and less capable students were going to learn the new math. Agreeing with the mathematicians' own favorable assess-ment of their efforts, the NSF granted SMSG an additional $1,184,000, and in 1961, SMSG's Advisory Board voted to have SMSG "continue indefinitely."

Activities mounted. A fourth summer writing session in 1961 pro-duced completed elementary school textbooks and revised secondary texts. By fall 1961, school orders of SMSG textbooks for grades seven through twelve had reached over 500,000. Over the next few years, SMSG prepared a series of materials for teachers and a collection of monographs for mathematically talented students; revised its origi-nal textbooks; added materials for kindergarten through third grade; translated the secondary school textbooks into Spanish for use in Puerto Rico; experimented with the development of texts for programmed learning; and established a film center to create films for classroom use and teacher in-service training.

SMSG had undertaken the development of textbooks with the understanding that it would remain in the textbook business only until such time as commercial publishers had incorporated the new content and approaches into their own offerings. SMSG did not see itself as replacing the commercial publishing industry. According to Ed Begle, SMSG's contribution lay in providing publishers with a "concrete example of the kind of curriculum that we thought both feasible and appropriate for today's children."[5] Throughout the 1960s and early 1970s, the commercial publishers moved quickly to develop textbooks in line with the widely publicized "modern" approach. As they did so, SMSG turned its attention to other areas, attempting to develop experimental curricula and to sponsor research in school mathematics.

From the outset, SMSG had been interested in assessing the effec-tiveness of its new materials. In 1962, SMSG launched a large-scale evaluation, the National Longitudinal Study of Mathematical Achievement, which followed more than 120,000 students over five years of mathematical study. Completed in 1967, the study produced a mixed picture. Students who had used the SMSG series performed somewhat better in areas of comprehension, analysis, and application – exactly the areas that had most concerned the curriculum reformers. But mathematics education traditionally involved computation, the relatively simple skills of adding, subtracting, dividing, and multiplying numbers. Here the Longitudinal Study was less positive: The students who used SMSG appeared slightly less able to handle computation than those who had used more traditional textbooks. Reviewers of the study pulled back from reaching definitive conclusions, arguing that a comparison of the outcomes of the different approaches to mathematics was "exceedingly difficult and complex, leading to few generalizations." Other tests, however, found similar results: Students using the SMSG tests usually scored higher on conceptual measures and lower on computation measures than students exposed to other textbook series. Surveying these results, one mathematician concluded, "a modern schoolboy knows that the sum of two natural numbers is a natural number, but he doesn't know which one!"[6]

By the time the Longitudinal Study was completed in 1967, the whole experiment in mathematics curriculum reform had become controversial. Reactions of mathematicians, mathematics teachers, and parents to the new math curriculum ranged from strong endorsement to harsh condemnation. The mathematics community was itself divided on the merits of the new curriculum. Many mathematicians were enthusiastic about the SMSG texts; although the texts were not perfect, they believed that the content and approach were vastly superior to those of previous textbooks. Opponents argued that the SMSG curriculum was too abstract, that it did not provide enough examples of practical applications of mathematics, and that it was appropriate only for students who would pursue careers in mathematics or mathematics-based disciplines.

Many teachers were also apprehensive about the new approach to mathematics instruction. Their lack of enthusiasm took the curriculum reformers by surprise. The early users of the texts, both teachers and students, had responded very favorably to the new presentation of material. In 1965, William Wooton wrote that "almost all of the teachers who have used SMSG textbooks look upon them as presenting significantly better mathematics, in a much more meaningful manner, than those to which they had been accustomed."[7] As the new texts were distributed more widely, however, they met with greater criticism. In order to teach the new math, teachers had to learn new vocabulary and concepts. The new mathematics curriculum also required teachers to assume a new role in the classroom. In place of the structure of the conventional mathematics lesson – teacher explanation followed by student exercises – the new curriculum called for an open exchange between teachers and students. Mathematics learning, which had traditionally been based on right and wrong answers and right and wrong ways to arrive at those answers, became open to negotiation. Neither the answers nor the approach used to derive them was certain. The new approach emphasized variety, questioning, and criticism as essential to understanding.

This new instructional format ran into direct conflict with what Seymour Sarason described as the "highly overlearned attitudes and ways of thinking" that many teachers had about teaching mathematics. Teachers, Sarason reported, had mixed reactions. Although many were caught up in the enthusiasm, intellectual stimulation, novelty, and prestige of the new math, many were also worried about their ability to teach it. "They became increasingly anxious as it became increasingly clear that the new math was indeed new (to most of them), that learning it to a criterion of security was not going to be easy, and that summer workshops of five weeks' duration might expose their insecurity and, in the case of some, their inadequacy."[8] Teachers who did not have summer training in the use of SMSG or did not have access to curriculum supervisors familiar with the new curriculum, as many did not, found the new textbooks especially difficult to use. The textbooks posed particular problems for elementary school teachers, who usually had limited training in mathematics. The SMSG elementary texts varied the most from the traditional curriculum, introducing new concepts such as sets, nondecimal bases, prime numbers, and factors.

If the new math was confusing to many teachers, it was even more bewildering to parents. What *was* this new math, and why was it superior to the arithmetic they had been taught? Parents' skepticism turned to frustration and irritation when they found themselves unable to assist their children with their homework. Many could not make any sense of it and found their children's discussions of their mathematics classes almost incomprehensible. Comedian-songwriter and MIT mathematics professor Tom Lehrer captured their feelings:

> Some of you who have small children may
> have perhaps been in the embarrassing position
> of being unable to do your child's arithmetic homework
> because of the current revolution in mathematics
> teaching known as "new math". . . .
>
> In the new approach, the important thing is to
> understand what you're doing rather than to
> get the right answer.
>
> Hooray for new math, hooray for new math.
> It won't do you a bit of good to read new math.
> It's so simple, so very simple, that only a child can do it.[9]

By the end of the 1960s, the new math was in retreat. In part, like many of the curriculum reform efforts of the 1950s and early 1960s, it was a victim of a shift in priorities toward compensatory learning that marked the debates over equality during the second half of the decade. This shift resulted in a de facto turning away from intellectual rigor. But the new math reformers also misunderstood the process of changing schools. SMSG had begun with the best and the brightest: top-flight mathematicians and mathematics teachers from the best high schools in the country. They wrote curriculum for the most capable secondary school students, those most likely to carry their mathematics lessons into advanced mathematics and science courses at the universities, and then into mathematics and science careers. On the heels of this success, the less academically able and the young would receive attention. Success at the top would spill over to those at the bottom.

Such an approach would have been controversial no matter what the curriculum content was. Once local school districts had to make hard choices about where to spend their funds, the academic elitism of the mathematics programs would undoubtedly become a target. But the nature of the new mathematics itself seriously violated what many believed schools, and school mathematics in particular, were supposed to be doing. The reformers' enthusiasm for the radical postwar era changes in mathematics was not shared or understood by the general public. Lay people and educators continued to assume that mathematics, first and foremost, meant computation and practical applications. They were confused and bothered by the emphasis on abstract mathematics in the new math texts. The mathematics reformers wanted to revolutionize mathematics teaching. But the revolution was not to be.

The new math reformers underestimated how difficult it was to change the culture of the school. For thousands of mathematics teachers, many of whom knew very little advanced mathematics, the curriculum reforms required extraordinary efforts to learn the new material and adopt new teaching methods. Teachers were usually expected to learn and teach under the same working conditions that had always made drill, simple-to-mark workbooks and worksheets, and standard textbooks attractive teaching techniques. Principals and teachers became skeptical about the worth and practicality of the new curriculum. They were confused about what the new math meant; cautious about, if not antagonistic to, reforms that increased their work load and required them to change their teaching; and defensive about the growing complaints from parents and students. Increasingly, they returned to the familiar format and content of traditional textbooks. Although some new mathematics concepts found their way into these commercial texts, the most popular textbooks were far more traditional. The enthusiasm for mathematics reform of those summer months in 1958–62 had been extraordinary. It seemed, for that brief period, that the commitment to the new curriculum would be infectious. Less than a decade later, however, both the enthusiasm and the commitment had disappeared.

MAN: A COURSE OF STUDY (MACOS)

As the new mathematics and science curricula were being nationally distributed in the 1960s, scholars in other academic disciplines were designing new instructional programs in their subject areas. The social studies unit *Man: A Course of Study (MACOS)* was produced during this second expanded phase of curriculum development. The impetus for the curriculum evolved out of the earlier mathematics and science projects. The curriculum was distributed in the 1960s and in the 1970s became the focus of national controversy.[10]

In 1962, the staff of Educational Services, Inc. (ESI),* a nonprofit organization created by the developers of the Physical Science Study

---

* In 1967, ESI became the Educational Development Center (EDC). To avoid confusion, the name ESI is used throughout this chapter.

Committee, received a grant from the Ford Foundation to begin work on a "Social Studies and Humanities Program." Some ESI scholars wanted to start designing new curriculum materials immediately; others thought that they should first articulate a coherent conceptual framework for social studies education. Proceeding along the former course, Harvard anthropologist Douglas Oliver assembled a team to begin developing a curriculum for grades one through six. He commissioned the preparation of two film series, one of the Netsilik Eskimos of Northern Canada and one of baboons in African game parks. The films were intended to place students in the role of ethnographer; they showed the culture of the Eskimos and the behavior of the baboons without any commentary, leaving students to interpret the actions themselves. Meanwhile, a second group of scholars, led by Jerome Bruner, attempted to write an intellectual prospectus derived from the social sciences for the new ESI social studies unit.

The first of the curricula produced under Oliver's supervision, a unit on the origin of cities, was field tested and evaluated in 1963 and 1964. In the fall of 1964, Oliver turned over the leadership of the ESI project to Bruner. This change in leadership meant a significant shift in the course of curriculum development. Whereas Oliver was largely anthropological in orientation, Bruner was interested in designing an interdisciplinary program. Whereas Oliver had set in motion the writing of units for grades one through six, Bruner focused on developing one ungraded unit directed at students in the upper elementary grades. In place of the heavy concentration on content in the Oliver units, Bruner sought a curriculum that would enhance general understanding of the social sciences and foster the development of cognitive skills.

Over the course of the 1964–5 academic year, the new social studies program began to take shape. Named *Man: A Course of Study,* the curriculum addressed three questions: "What is human about human beings? How did they get that way? How can they be made more so?"[11] The curriculum planners designed materials around five themes: social organization, language, belief systems, technology, and childhood. Once the materials were drafted, the MACOS course was ready to be tried in actual classrooms.

MACOS was tested in the summer of 1965 in an elementary school summer program in Newton, Massachusetts, widely considered one of the country's most sophisticated and preeminent school systems.

34

With almost as many staff members taking part in the summer school as students (sixty-one staff* to seventy-five students), every part of the program was duly recorded and extensively evaluated. Each morning, teachers taught pupils using the new course materials; each afternoon, the entire staff discussed the morning's experience; each evening, the curriculum team wrote and revised the next day's lesson plan. By the summer's end, the ESI staff had collected a massive amount of data on MACOS. The program had been intense, but it had also been exhilarating.

In the winter of 1965, the curriculum planners began a cycle of curriculum development and classroom teaching. Materials were designed, field tested, and then revised accordingly. At the same time, the training of teachers was begun under the direction of sociologist Anita Mishler of the ESI staff. Although ESI had originally planned for teacher training to begin after the curriculum was fully drafted, Mishler wanted to orient teachers to the curriculum's new content and pedagogy immediately and wanted this training to be simultaneous with the curriculum development. Up to that point, only a few teachers – for the most part individuals who were known to the Harvard and MIT faculty participating in the curriculum development – had been involved in discussions about MACOS.

During the spring of 1966, Mishler worked with two groups of teachers: fourteen experienced teachers from the Newton school system and ten student teachers from Lesley College in Cambridge, Massachusetts. With both groups, Mishler found that teachers were uncomfortable teaching MACOS. Not only was the subject matter entirely new to most teachers, but the open-ended format caused anxiety among many – a finding that replicated the new math experience. Because the MACOS curriculum ruled out prescribing what direction students' inquiries should take, each session was unpredictable. The teacher had to guide students' questions sensitively toward the lesson's conceptual objective. To teach MACOS effectively, teachers had to be thoroughly familiar with the subject matter and fully aware of the curriculum's conceptual aims. According to the MACOS teacher's guide, "a lesson plan is not a script . . . only a framework within which the most challenging work is still to be accomplished."[12]

---

*The sixty-one staff included seventeen teachers, twelve content scholars, seven research assistants, ten instructional researchers, four audiovisual specialists, and eleven administrators.

In 1966, the MACOS materials were tested in a second summer school program. Each classroom was staffed with one ESI head teacher and four teachers from the ESI teacher-training program (two experienced and two student teachers). Throughout the summer, a team of independent evaluators hired by ESI closely monitored the use of the curriculum. During the 1966–7 academic year, the information they gathered was used by the ESI staff to guide their revisions of the MACOS curriculum.

By the spring of 1967, the curriculum was complete. The first units examined animal behavior through the life cycle of the salmon and the behavior of herring gulls and baboons. Later units considered different human societies, focusing on the culture of the Netsilik Eskimos and the African Bushmen. The juxtaposition of animal and human behaviors served to illustrate their commonalities and the uniqueness of humans; the presentation of traditional societies showed how cultures developed by adapting to environmental conditions. Lessons were presented through ethnographic films, replicas of archeological objects, short stories, simulated diaries and anthropological handbooks, games, and textbooks.

With the curriculum materials in place, the ESI staff notified commercial publishers that the curriculum was available. ESI wanted to retain control over the content and design of MACOS. But their confidence about finding someone to accept these terms was shaken as publisher after publisher reviewed and rejected the curriculum. Publishers explained that the course content and pedagogy of MACOS would make it difficult to market, and that few schools were likely to substitute MACOS for the American history customarily taught in the fifth grade. They told the MACOS developers that their stress on inductive methods, small-group instruction, the teacher as participant rather than authority, and multimedia design were formidable obstacles to adoption by teachers. The publishers claimed, according to Peter Dow, that "teachers want *simple* programs . . . that are easy to teach and that require a minimum of preparation." The series, they believed, was potentially controversial and too costly – approximately $6,000 for a five-classroom set, eight times what schools usually spent on social studies material.[13]

The publishers painted a grim picture of curriculum improvement: school systems not interested in buying anything dramatically different; teachers only able to teach simple programs; no one wanting controversy. The premise of the MACOS reformers that publishing houses might be their allies in curriculum reform was wrong. By assuming that the creativity inherent in the new curriculum would sweep aside traditional social studies teaching, the reformers failed to recognize the constraints on school systems to institute major changes.

Even as ESI searched for a commercial publisher, a growing number of teachers requested the curriculum. Because of the reformers' belief that no teacher should use MACOS without being trained in the use of the curriculum materials, this meant an increased need for teacher training. But because of the complexity of the new social studies curriculum, exposing teachers to the content was not sufficient. As Mishler concluded, teachers needed "an occasion . . . to reexamine their assumptions about teaching, to rethink the role of schooling in society, and to participate in the process of educational change."[14] She drafted a "parallel curriculum" for teachers who were using MACOS to encourage them to reassess their pedagogical beliefs and approaches. But such a sophisticated program required considerable time to create and money to implement. In the meantime, more immediate needs had to be addressed.

To make MACOS available to more teachers, ESI ran training programs for workshop leaders in the summer of 1968 in Colorado, California, Washington, D.C., Pennsylvania, and Massachusetts. Their success led ESI to propose that MACOS dissemination, evaluation, and teacher training become decentralized. ESI encouraged participants to seek funds for regional training centers; a year later, eleven colleges and universities had received NSF funds to establish dissemination projects.

The dissemination efforts gained momentum as the search for a commercial publisher ground to a halt. An organization was needed that could develop a profit-sharing alternative to the dissemination system supported by the NSF. Several organizations expressed interest in this new arrangement; after careful consideration of two proposals, ESI decided to sign a contract with the Curriculum Development Associates of Washington, D.C.

In the fall of 1970, 918 teachers and 22,163 students were using MACOS. Although Mishler's parallel curriculum program could not be fully implemented for lack of funding, the ongoing ESI evaluations of MACOS indicated that dissemination was working well. A three-year comprehensive evaluation released in 1970 concluded that the MACOS curriculum was successfully accomplishing its objectives. "The materials," the report stated, "have revitalized the social studies classroom, and their integration with an interactive pedagogy seems to serve well the upper elementary grade youngsters for whom the course was designed." The final report of a Marin County, California, study of various "new social studies curricula" used in their schools found that "the curricular program developed by the Educational Development Center entitled *Man: A Course of Study* obtained responses far more positive than any other program that was widely tested." Still other evaluations in such scattered locations as Bellevue, Washington, Nashville, Tennessee, and Ashland, Oregon, gave the MACOS unit high marks. In 1969, the American Educational Research Association cited Jerome Bruner for his "leadership in coordinating the work of other scholars, classroom teachers, media specialists, and curriculum developers to produce the fifth-grade, multi-media program *Man: A Course of Study*." The citation quoted one evaluator who considered MACOS "one of the most important efforts of our time to relate research findings and theory in educational psychology to the development of new and better instructional materials." These accolades gratified the reformers.[15]

The story of the MACOS curriculum was far from over, however. The first indication of problems came in 1970 when a Lake City, Florida, group, calling itself "Citizens for Moral Education," accused the MACOS curriculum of favoring "sex education, evolution, hippie-yippie philosophy, pornography, gun control, and communism," and demanded that it be removed from classroom use immediately.[16] The anti-MACOS group held meetings, distributed leaflets, and purchased time on a local radio program. In response, the Lake City School Board listened to arguments for and against the curriculum and decided that instruction in MACOS should be made elective and that a traditional social studies course should be made available to those who opted out of MACOS classes. Forty-five of the 360 students taking the course asked to transfer from MACOS to the traditional course; the following year, MACOS was dropped from school offerings altogether.

The Florida debate had barely ended when another began in Montgomery County, Maryland. Although the attacks against MACOS in Maryland were less fiery than those in Florida, the Maryland skirmish suggested that the Florida fight was not a rare, isolated event. In 1971, MACOS came under attack in Phoenix, Arizona, where, Dow argues, opponents treated the curriculum "as an alien intrusion on established ways of thinking about American society, as a subversive program designed to undermine the values inherent in familiar textbook courses like *The Free and the Brave.*" Before long, debates over the use of MACOS spread to other school districts, including Bellevue, Washington; Burlington, Vermont; and Corinth, New York. With each attack, opposition grew more vehement and more sophisticated. Whereas early critics had accused MACOS of all ills from atheism to communism, the later attacks focused on the social studies curriculum's content, pedagogy, and underlying assumptions. Critics from different localities shared information and joined forces. A growing professional network of MACOS teachers was matched by an emerging network of opposition to the curriculum.

In 1976 the controversy over MACOS moved onto the national stage. In the U.S. Congress, Arizona Congressman John Conlan questioned a line item of $110,000 to fund "informational workshops" for MACOS in the NSF's budget. Conlan argued that the federal government should not finance a curriculum "designed to mold children's social attitudes and beliefs along lines that are almost always at variance with the beliefs and social values of their parents and local communities." Furthermore, he said, the federal government should not finance curriculum development at all, because, by doing so, it placed itself in direct competition with the commercial publishing industry.

Conlan's position was supported by many local groups as well as by several national associations, most prominent being the Council for Basic Education and the Heritage Foundation. In response to Conlan's charges, the House of Representatives, Committee on Science and Technology, established a review subcommittee; the NSF initiated its own internal review of the MACOS curriculum; and the General Accounting Office began an investigation of ESI's use of funding for MACOS. When the issue of funding came to a vote, several congressmen took strong pro-MACOS positions. Others argued against Conlan on the grounds that Congress should not set itself up as a censor. After considerable discussion in both the House and the Senate, the MACOS appropriation was passed.

In time, MACOS was cleared by all federal review bodies. But the damage had been done. The fight over the curriculum had consumed time and money. It brought MACOS a national notoriety that made school administrations skittish about using the curriculum in their own communities. The NSF provided no further funding to ESI or to Curriculum Development Associates for work on the MACOS curriculum. Although the dissemination of MACOS continued, the development of the social studies curriculum had come to an end.*

It would be easy to read the story of MACOS as a classic conflict between cosmopolitans and parochials, between those willing to cast their net broadly to understand human society and those whose values are too narrow to allow the introduction of comparative studies and open-ended questions into the curriculum. But to do so would be to simplify the complexity of the conflicts over values that MACOS wrought. The designers of MACOS wanted to transform the content and teaching of social studies. In the process, they uncovered value-laden problems that went far beyond the scope of the issues they were tackling. MACOS was accused, for instance, of being irreligious; it was also attacked for being racist. When the nation's new social agendas heightened the sensitivity to racial issues, the designers of MACOS dropped the unit on the African Bushmen from their curriculum, believing it "politically unwise to introduce materials abut partially naked, 'dark-skinned primitives' into the classroom." Critics of MACOS saw the curriculum as promoting "cultural relativism and environmental determinism." Textbooks should attempt to be neutral, they argued, or should present a balance of values, rather than one perspective only.[17]

But objections to MACOS were not only about its potentially sensitive material. Many parents and scholars shared the concerns of the Council on Basic Education, the Heritage Foundation, and others that the use of MACOS in the fifth grade occurred at the expense of U.S. history, the subject matter traditionally taught in that grade. Although the interdisciplinary curriculum might be interesting, they argued, students needed to be provided, first, with a solid grounding in history, civics, and geography. MACOS, they felt, deemphasized facts and skills. A different set of values was at issue: which subject matter was more valuable, which content deserved priority, and, even more basic, what educational purpose was a course of study to serve?

Like the new mathematics curriculum, MACOS raised problems for teachers. To use MACOS, teachers had to learn new subject matter; they had to spend considerable time preparing for each class, getting the various materials in order, determining the probable flow

---

*MACOS is still being distributed by Curriculum Development Associates, Inc. in Washington, D.C. It is available in two formats: the original or full program and a somewhat shorter basic course.

of student questions, and deciding the best means of guiding class discussions. The emphasis on open-ended discussion, on relativism in evaluating the behaviors under study, and on problem solving required different classroom practices. Many teachers greeted these changes enthusiastically. But many others found it easier to retain the old, familiar textbooks, particularly when they were faced with the demands of a newly diverse student population. When teachers were given little time, little incentive, and little payoff for changing their teaching practice and course content, it was difficult for any curriculum reform to gain much ground.

MACOS was also unlucky. It appeared just as the era of curriculum reform was coming to a close. When further development in other social studies areas became necessary, federal support for curriculum change diminished. Funding for the parallel curriculum for teacher training never materialized. Local school systems facing tightening budgets were less able to draw upon federal funds for the purchase and upkeep of materials.

There is a special irony to the story of MACOS, for it fell victim to two problems it originally hoped to counter. First, to satisfy growing demands for "relevance" in the curriculum, MACOS presented students with concrete experiences of animals and humans rather than traditional history and social studies courses. Yet, as social studies courses began to focus on the immediate concerns of civil rights and the Vietnam War, MACOS seemed both too tame and too abstract.

The second irony is that MACOS was a victim of the emerging conflict between equality and excellence. MACOS drew heavily upon Jerome Bruner's assertion that "any subject can be taught effectively in some intellectually honest form to any child at any stage of development."[18] By that, Bruner meant that the critical concepts and structures that underlie disciplines and problems could be communicated to all students. Pedagogically, MACOS was designed to cut across grade levels and to be taught in classrooms with students of diverse abilities, backgrounds, and interests. In practice, however, MACOS came to be seen as a strongly academic program that depended upon high levels of basic literacy skills, comprehension, and analytic abilities – in both teachers and students – and it appealed most to those already used to thinking in terms of a world beyond their immediate communities. By the early 1970s, however, public debate about learning had come to define such a curriculum as elitist – a position that MACOS innovators had initially tried to counter.

With school budgets growing tight, investment in programs was hard to justify. Adding a potentially controversial program to already politicized schools made little sense. In the end, MACOS smacked of much of the elitism that affected the SMSG curriculum, despite the fervent hopes of its originators that it would not.

REFLECTIONS ON CURRICULUM REFORM

In less than two decades, the enthusiasm for a curriculum revolution that began in the early 1950s was gone. The authors of SMSG, MACOS, and the other curriculum reform efforts in the sciences, languages, and humanities had sought a major transformation in what was learned and how it was taught. Many teachers were exposed to new approaches to teaching; many capitalized on the reforms by incorporating into their classes those aspects they judged relevant. Traditional textbooks incorporated some of the new content and format. By severely challenging the existing curriculum, the reformers of the 1950s and early 1960s prepared the way for the later proliferation of curriculum choices. Paradoxically, they made it easier to adopt a cafeteria-style curriculum.

But neither the curriculum nor teaching was transformed in the way the reformers intended. In commenting on a 1979 NSF evaluation of science, mathematics, and social studies curricula, the National Council of Teachers of Mathematics concluded that there was "reason to question the extent to which any of the proposals for innovative pedagogy have influenced predominant instructional patterns." Most mathematics classes involved pretty much what they always had: extensive teacher-directed explanation and questioning, textbook authorities, and student seatwork on pencil-and-paper assignments. Overall, the NSF study found, mathematics was seen by teachers and students as "a dry, mechanical thing, to be done stoically."[19]

The evidence on social studies was similar. Most teachers used textbooks in traditional ways and did not draw upon the social sciences. The National Council for the Social Studies noted that, for the student, knowing was "largely a matter of having information; and the demonstration of the knowledge frequently involves being able to reproduce the language of the text in class discussions or on tests." Students in the 1970s were taught in basically the same way as their parents: textbook assignments followed by recitation.[20]

The new science curriculum materials met with somewhat more success than the new math and the new social studies. At the higher grade levels particularly, the new science materials had some lasting impact. Nevertheless, with the possible exception of the Biological Sciences Curriculum Study (BSCS), the new biology program, use of the new science curricula was far below that of the traditional science texts. The high expectations for foreign language instruction dissipated. Language laboratories deteriorated, and foreign languages almost entirely disappeared from the curriculum. The new English curriculum briefly flourished but quickly lost much of its academic content.

In trying to understand why, after the protracted efforts at curriculum reform, most subjects are still being taught in traditional ways, we find that several issues emerge. Each cuts across the particular curriculum reform efforts: competing claims over what ought to be learned, the relationship of reform to the culture of the school, and the shifting priorities of the educational system.

Whenever reformers set out to change curricula, they define, in effect, what they think ought to be learned in school. In the 1950s, with the best of intentions, reformers assumed that the best minds could agree on the best forms of knowledge, and there would be an end to the matter; the community at large would go along. They underestimated the extent to which local and family values excited deep feelings about what should be taught in schools. By the 1960s and 1970s, the onslaught of heated political controversies forced reformers to adopt more relative criteria about what should be learned. No one subject was held to be more important than another – there was no agreed-upon common core of knowledge. In this climate, it was easy to make the case for almost any innovation in the curriculum. Vague notions such as "student as teacher" and "community as teacher" were common. Some reformers even urged students to see themselves as oppressed by the schools and by the demands of a formal adult curriculum. These were not easy times for leading scholars who advanced concepts of knowledge that smacked of rigor or elitism.[21]

Because the reformers came from the nation's prestigious universities, they tended to model their curricula after the academic content of college and graduate courses. They were enthusiastic about academic research and highly critical of school instruction. Their goal was to teach young students the structure of their discipline, to have them think like mathematicians or social or natural scientists. They were less concerned about the realities of classroom teaching and more interested in intellectual discourse on the ideal instructional content. At best they were ambivalent toward school teachers. When they included teachers in designing curricula, they chose the best teachers from the best schools. They believed that most teachers were part of the problem. As Seymour Sarason suggests, "at least some of those pushing for change were of the opinion that not all of the inadequacies of the old math resided in the math *as such* but also reflected inadequacies of many teachers."[22]

Yet, the curriculum planners were dependent on these same teachers to implement their programs. The teachers were often less convinced of the wisdom of using the new curricula. The farther afield the curriculum was disseminated, the more difficult it was for the curriculum reformers to transmit the intellectual excitement of the programs to those who had not participated in their creation. For many teachers, the approach of the new curricula seemed directed toward those students who were already excelling; the new instructional formats undermined the traditional means of maintaining discipline in the classroom.

Parents, school boards, and local citizens did not always agree with professional prescriptions of what was best for their children. This clash of values, which has been a persistent feature of American educational history, resurfaced in the disputes over MACOS. The clash had not been unintended. The curriculum designers had expressly sought to offer pupils new insights and perspectives: scientific objectivity, the evolutionary nature of humans, and cultural relativism. But their curriculum had little room for maneuver or compromise, nor did they foresee the intensity of feeling that value differences would arouse.

Academic scholars themselves seriously disagreed over the worth of the new curricula. The new math raised questions that have persisted throughout the history of mathematics about the emphasis that should be placed on the development of students' understanding of mathematical concepts, and about the amount of attention that should be given to the applications of mathematics versus abstraction and generalization. The new social studies similarly became part of the ongoing debate within the profession about the proper definition, purposes, and content of social studies education. It raised

44

questions about the proper content of social studies: history, civics, or social sciences, or some combination thereof.[23]

Finally, the new curricula were affected by the consequences of a shift in societal values. The new mathematics and science curricula came into being because of Cold War-based concerns about the nation's scientific and technological capabilities. They were directed toward those gifted students deemed most likely to pursue careers in science and mathematics-based fields. In today's terms, they were propelled by a desire for excellence. But no sooner had the curricula appeared than the national agenda began to shift. As equality and the demands of the disadvantaged captured the nation's attention in the 1960s, the structure and content of schooling were once again reexamined. Whereas investment of substantial resources in mathematics and science instruction for gifted students seemed to make good sense when the development of technological expertise was the objective, this expenditure was seen as elitist and discriminatory when equality was the goal. In the new drive for equality, the pursuit of excellence became less fashionable. To some commentators, the results were disastrous: "Excellence in science education was attained when it was important enough to society; but mediocrity returned when concern was withdrawn."[24]

This tension between excellence and equality is deeply embedded in American educational history, and we will return to it in more detail in the following chapters. Many of the curriculum reformers of the 1950s, like Jerome Bruner, tried to resolve the tension. They believed that all students could learn more than they were currently learning, and blamed inadequate curricula and poor teaching. But at the same time, they wanted to produce an intellectual and technological elite to maintain America's competitive edge. They were also eager to have their experiments in curriculum development confirmed by the most capable students.

As the curriculum reforms gained national attention, their focus on the brightest students came under scrutiny. Despite the hope of many of the reformers that their curricula, based on developmental psychology, interdisciplinary problem solving, and creative pedagogy, would be used by all students, they had not counted on how crucial teachers were to any curriculum. Nor were they aware that programs for the most advanced students would be implemented at the expense of the disadvantaged. The excellence sought in the new curricula became, in practice, tied to inequalities. When, in the mid-1960s, the focus of educational policy became more avowedly committed to equality, the curriculum reforms that stressed excellence found themselves peripheral.

PART II
THE PURPOSES OF SCHOOLING

3

EQUALITY AND INEQUALITY

The challenge to American education is to be both equal and excellent. Unless we seek equality, we undermine the possibility of achieving the excellence that comes when all students fulfill their learning capacities. Unless we seek excellence, our notion of equality will be barren, for it will lack a commitment to quality. Achieving equality and excellence involves providing opportunities so that each student can do his or her best, succeed at something worthwhile, and take pride in that accomplishment. This is probably as close as we can get to an educational "right."

In the twentieth century, we have tended to focus on either equality or excellence. The period of curricular reform of the 1950s and 1960s, when the predominant concern was for excellence in education, was followed by a period of emphasis on equality of educational opportunity. Blacks, whites, and Hispanics formed coalitions to fight for the equalization of school financing, the integration of schools, the provision of compensatory education, and the introduction of English as a second language (ESL) and other special-need programs. They sought equality of access and treatment for those groups of students previously denied the full benefits of the American educational system.

In the 1980s, the call once again is for excellence in education. Many Americans now believe that the efforts to create a more egalitarian educational system were made at the expense of quality. Some believe that liberalizing the curriculum to serve a plurality of interests resulted in a permissiveness that converted learning into playing and "doing one's own thing." The calamitous decline in the number of students taking science, mathematics, and foreign language courses and the steady drop in SAT scores during the 1970s seem to support this view.

Many advocates of continuing and expanding efforts in support of equality acknowledge that educational standards may have deteriorated. But they fear that the renewed call for excellence may become a codeword for the reintroduction of discriminatory practices that unduly harm those who most need special attention. They see in the push for higher meritocratic standards, largely defined in terms of standardized test scores, a potential attack on nonwhites and the poor. The call for excellence in a period of limited and declining resources seems to have all the earmarks of rewarding some groups at the expense of others, only this time rewarding those who are already doing well.

Much of the present discussion about schools seems predicated on the assumption that ours is an either/or choice – either excellence or equality. Oversimplifications about the effects of the drive for either equality or excellence can do considerable harm because they tend to divide groups that share a common interest in the improvement of our schools. Equality and excellence in education need not be at odds. They will be in tension because they represent very different values. Their definition will be confusing and uncertain; their implementation will be controversial. But equality and excellence are both essential to public schooling in a democratic society. Where standards are compromised, where all students are not challenged, encouraged, or allowed to achieve their very best, they lose a critical opportunity that in many cases only schooling can give them.

POLITICAL EQUALITY, ECONOMIC INEQUALITY

The current antagonism between equality and excellence was not an issue for some mid-nineteenth-century advocates of the common school. In a less complex world than ours, they sought to open schools to all in order to disseminate knowledge as widely as possible. In 1830 the Working Men's Committee of Philadelphia argued that "the original element of despotism is a monopoly of talent, which consigns the multitude to comparative ignorance, and secures the balance of knowledge on the side of the rich and the rulers." Education would break this monopoly and, through equal access to knowledge, would be the "only security for equal liberty." Since there could be "no real liberty without a wide diffusion of real intelligence," all members of society had to be instructed alike in the nature and character of their equal rights and duties as human beings and as citizens.[1]

A somewhat similar perception that equality in education would enhance knowledge and thus further extend political equality was apparent when, in the 1840s, black parents in Boston petitioned the Boston School Committee for the right to send their children to integrated schools. High standards of learning were undermined, they argued, when certain groups in the population were thought unable to learn as well as others. Inequality, whether in access, funding, or curriculum, meant that both white and black children received less than their due.[2]

Not all nineteenth-century Americans believed that equality of access meant enhancement of learning. Many doubted the learning capacities of poor people, nonwhites, immigrants, and women. But the vision of those who fought for equality of access and treatment was a vision that articulated a close tie between equality and excellence. As the Working Men's Committee implied, both equality and excellence were necessary for citizenship; a citizenship based on limited knowledge was second-class citizenship.

Nineteenth-century common school advocates fought for and achieved tremendous victories in enhancing educational opportunity. They believed that equality in schooling increased everyone's moral sensibilities and political responsibilities. Public education was for citizenship. Americans often engaged in controversy over how citizens should behave, and many had a sense that some citizens should make more decisions than others. But they were acutely aware that all citizens in a democratic society could participate in governance, and that full participation depended upon moral judgments, understanding, knowledge, and commitment to the political process. Even as the particular ingredients of an education for citizenship changed over time, as greater levels of literacy became necessary, for example, Americans understood that mass education and egalitarian citizenship were inextricably linked. Before the twentieth century, not everyone was considered a citizen, but those who were were entitled to sufficient schooling for democratic participation. On that basis, aspirations for equality of access to schooling were closely linked to concerns for democratic politics.[3]

Economic inequality pushed in a different direction, however. Unlike the political equality accorded citizens, the outcome of economic competition was presumed to be economic inequality. Citizens competed in the marketplace for individual and private gains.

Equal as citizens, they were unequal as economic beings. The two assumptions coexisted in an uneasy relationship to one another. Even de Tocqueville, who emphasized the high degree of political and economic equality in the America of the 1830s, was aware of the tension and warned that the growth of a commercial aristocracy and the existence of slavery threatened democracy.

Nineteenth-century schools were not directly involved in establishing economic roles. Schooling was for citizenship and carried political and moral obligations. One did not have to graduate from school or be certified by taking a requisite set of courses to enter occupations. The school was not considered responsible for economic inequalities – except among those groups like the Working Men's Committee, which associated access to knowledge generally with greater economic opportunity.[4]

In the decades after 1880, many of these values changed. The growth of industrial capitalism led to a reformulation of perceptions about public schooling. The moral and political terms that had dominated nineteenth-century discussions of education gave way to technical and economic terms. Slowly at first, but with increasing rapidity as the twentieth century progressed, this shift changed the spirit in which Americans went to school, as educational achievement became critical in the race for economic and social attainment.

This shift in the purpose of schooling meant that staying in school became the measure of what one would do afterward. With competition for economic places channeled into school attendance and achievement, students competed for advancement up the educational ladder. Mass elementary schooling was followed by mass secondary schooling. That, in turn, was followed by pressure for mass higher education in the post–World War II period. Increasingly, educators, parents, and students themselves phrased the primary justification of schooling in vocational and economic terms: Stay in school because it will help you get a better job.

At the same time, the internal dynamics of schooling shifted to a new emphasis on how to differentiate students rather than on how to teach them in common. Going to junior high school was a process of being sorted into academic, vocational, and general tracks. The seemingly scientific measurements of intelligence reinforced the process by suggesting that some could learn a great deal and prepare for positions of leadership, whereas others could not. From the latter group, the educational system should not expect too much.

As the rationale for public schooling shifted, the political ends of schooling were subordinated to the economic ones. Equality in education was redefined as equality of opportunity in an economically inegalitarian society. In preparation for their different occupational roles as adults, high school students were exposed to different curricula, thus providing the justification for the comprehensive curriculum of twentieth-century schools. Equality under this doctrine no longer meant equal exposure to a common curriculum.[5]

The new responsibility of the schools to prepare youths for their unequal places in the economic system did not eliminate the schools' political responsibility to prepare citizens who were, in theory, equal. But it did sharpen the dilemma of what schools ought to emphasize. How would the ends of political equality and economic inequality be balanced within the educational system? The dilemma had profound significance for the debate over equality and excellence. Once preparation for economic inequality became the predominant concern of the educational system – dominating, not replacing, the older political purposes of the schools – excellence became defined by economic payoffs. By the middle of the twentieth century, schools that seemed to lead to high economic returns or high-status occupations were considered "excellent." Courses that led to the elite colleges were "excellent."

This was a disturbing but logical outcome of the dominance of economic motivations in schooling. It made an economic difference whether one obtained access to the college preparatory, as opposed to the vocational or general, track in high school. It made an economic difference if one gained access to the four-year state university rather than the community college. It made an economic difference whether one attended an elite private university or not. How much or even what one actually learned in the academic track, or in the state university, or in the elite private college was less important economically than just getting there. No wonder that, when the drive for equality expanded in the 1960s, it focused on those features of the educational system that limited access to programs that paid off. Because the educational system had become the primary route to occupations, eliminating the most immediate roadblocks mattered most. If grades or standardized tests were roadblocks, eliminate them; if segregation was a roadblock, stop it; if science or mathematics

courses were roadblocks, avoid them. It was easy, and quite under-
standable, to evaluate all educational issues in terms of their effects
on occupational opportunities.

PURSUING EQUALITY

We need to begin by recognizing that equality is a complex goal,
ambiguous and indeterminate both conceptually and in implementation. If we acknowledge how problematic equality is, how much it
depends on people's interests, motivations, and capacities, and how
varied the ends of education are, it is hard to imagine a time when
we can say that we have achieved equality in education. To insist on
establishing a unitary and fixed standard is to pursue a chimera that
will only frustrate us, and probably further divide us, as we pursue
egalitarian measures with ambiguous results.

The focus of all efforts at achieving equality in education should
be on learning. John Dewey's discussion of growth offers a useful
approach for thinking about equality and learning. In *Democracy and
Education,* he argues that learning should not be seen as having a
fixed end. All stages of learning should be marked by growth. The
experience of learning enhances the likelihood of our learning still
more. The more one learns, the more one wants to learn and the
more one is capable of learning.[6]

Equality is not static. Like learning, it is marked by growth. As we
pursue equality, we change our definitions and enlarge our aspirations. Because equality does not have fixed ends, but involves growth,
we need guiding principles to inform our actions. Two principles
ought to be paramount.

First, equality recognizes different capabilities and different interests. Rather than being an attempt to make everyone the same, the
commitment to equality acknowledges, in Michael Walzer's words,
"the range and variety of human capacities: intelligence, physical
strength, agility and grace, artistic creativity, mechanical skill, leadership, endurance, memory, psychological insight, the capacity for
hard work – even moral strength, sensitivity, the ability to express
compassion."[7] Equality in America requires accommodation of a
variety of principles. In education, it means taking account of the
fullest possible range of issues: financing; pedagogy and curriculum;
racial, class, and gender status; organizational structures; and occupational outcomes and economic returns. All of these issues have

been, and will continue to be, hotly contested. But in the debates, we ought not to lose our focus on learning.

Second, children should not be victimized because of their parents' disadvantages. Children whose parents lack money should not be denied access to health care, housing, nutritious food, or education. Every child or every family will not make the same use of those opportunities. But equality in education requires that the school be committed to play some role in reducing the obstacles to learning that derive from parental disadvantages. Economic inequalities may or may not be alleviated by the reduction of these obstacles; direct action in the economy and politics is undoubtedly more effective in promoting economic equality than the indirect effects of schooling. Overcoming the obstacles to learning is an appropriate and valid responsibility of schooling. Where schools have the effect, intended or otherwise, of exacerbating these obstacles, they are working against equality.

TRACKING AND INEQUALITY

No school practice undermines equality more than the tracking of students. Tracking takes many forms. The most prominent is caused by residential segregation, with students divided largely by class and race. Indeed, de facto and de jure residential segregation have become the most prevalent denial of the common school ideal. Within schools, tracking is of several kinds. In elementary grades, ability grouping is most often done by a single classroom teacher. At the junior high and high school levels, tracking occurs by assignment to differing ability levels of individual classes (English A, B, or C) or selection of a course of study (college preparatory, vocational, or general). However tracking is done at the secondary level, the separation of students is virtually complete. Few students move between tracks. Although, by European standards, the American system of tracking by likely vocational roles may seem limited, tracking in American schools reflects socioeconomic and racial divisions in the society: Lower-income and minority students are disproportionately enrolled in vocational curriculum and lower-track classes.[8]

For many students, being placed into tracks also means being limited to courses that are much less demanding and significantly less rich in content than they have a right to expect. A section of a state curriculum guide for a lower-tracked class, for example, expects students in history to be able to name three causes of the 1930s Depression and to list the order in which wars were fought. These expectations are depressingly low, devoid of any concern with analytic skills. Curricular expectations such as these imply that analytic skills are not needed, even if the students could be presumed to master them. Yet, facts to be memorized and regurgitated, not analyzed or interpreted, are not likely to be learned, or if learned, are unlikely to have any meaning beyond themselves. A curriculum composed exclusively or even predominantly of such items will have little meaning for either students or their teachers. Unless students are asked to do something with the list of causes for the Depression, the facts will be inert. Certainly, if neither student nor teacher is expected to think about how knowledge of historical events can be used to enhance citizenship, to give a sense of the past, to stimulate inquiry, or to understand antecedents to their own lives and situations, it is hard to see what the purposes of education are.

Contrast these minimal expectations to Philip Jackson's observations of an advanced class in a good school: "Students were encouraged to think on their own and to make up their own minds about things. They were encouraged, too, to be critical, albeit in a kindly manner, of the opinions of their classmates, of their teachers, and of the books and materials they were working with."[9] The distinction between what is expected of students in lower-track and advanced classes exists because only the best and brightest are thought to need critical habits and skills.

Even more powerful findings about tracking and its effects are presented in John Goodlad's study of thirty-eight schools and over 17,000 students. The study revealed significant differences between high-track (i.e., college-preparatory) and low-track (non-college-preparatory) classes. In the high track, more time was devoted to "higher-level cognitive processes": making judgments, drawing inferences, effecting syntheses, and using symbolism. In the low track, more time was given to rote learning and direct application of knowledge and skills. High-track classes used richer, more varied instructional materials than low-track classes. High-track classes were exposed more often to advantageous teaching practices than were low-track classes.[10]

The shame of American education is that all students are not expected to develop the skills of reason, communication, and literacy, and the habits of commitment and participation necessary for full citizenship in a democracy. The expectation of minimal learning is especially shameful when it is based on the presumption that many students lack the capacity to develop these skills, and that the largest proportion of those presumed to lack those capacities are nonwhite and lower-class. These "terminal" students in high school are presumed to have little need for these skills. Their minimal education, so the argument goes, is appropriate to the "reality" of their condition. The presumptions, and the arguments justifying them, set up an unbreakable cycle of low expectations and low achievement.

But the shame spills over to the whole educational system. In asking less of the low-track students, we set up the conditions whereby less is asked of the high-track students. The minimalist expectations for those at the bottom flow upward, and the corruption becomes pervasive.

We want to be clear here. We are not engaging in a wholesale attack on all forms of grouping. Our notion of equality does not mean that all students should be treated the same. Students have different interests, learning styles, and abilities. Some take considerable time to master a skill or learn a subject; others do so rapidly. It is important to acknowledge and take advantage of these differences in grouping students and in organizing curricula and teaching. Similarly, we are not opposed to all forms of education that aid youth in preparing for vocational roles. Asking students to think about occupations, to be aware of options before them, and to assess what they need to do to gain access to certain occupational roles can widen their own thinking about careers and enhance their understanding of the world of work. But to claim that the stereotypical program divisions – academic, vocational, commercial, and general – enhance knowledge about work and academic subject matter is a charade.

Thomas Green offers a relevant insight into our meaning. Suppose, Green writes, some children are "persuaded" early on to take business arithmetic, and, as a consequence, forfeit the chance to take algebra. "What is wrong about this," Green argues, "is not merely that it throws up artificial barriers to educational progress and thus unfairly predetermines the social destiny of youth." It is also wrong because it prepares youths for a decent life neither in business, nor in industry, nor in the crafts. "What is wrong, in short, is not that there is tracking, but that there is a denial of educational excellence."[11]

It has been surprisingly difficult to convince people of the limits of tracking, in part because the debate has most often centered on the issue of vocational education rather than on learning. Vocational education took shape in the early twentieth century by identifying itself with the democratization of access to secondary schooling and with the assertion of schooling's economic relevance. Vocational education was articulated as democratic education, committed to expanding and diversifying the curriculum, to basing course content on students' interests, and to making instruction relevant to economic goals. The resulting opposition between the academics and vocationalists has continued to dominate discussions of vocational education. To oppose vocational education is to open oneself to charges of academic elitism, to a willingness to impose uninteresting and irrelevant subject matter on youths, to hostility to manual labor, and to opposition to the economic returns that youths desire from their schooling.

There is a certain amount of truth in this. Many people turn their noses up at a vocational education as something for the masses but hardly appropriate for their children. Like being tracked in the low groups, vocational education courses are often thought of as something for "other people's" children, but not for "my" college-bound child. In contrast, students who dislike or are not doing well in academic courses find vocational programs attractive. They compare the dreariness and remoteness of their academic work with the potential benefits of their vocational courses. It is thus easy to see how academic and vocational programs are set against one another.

The use of schooling for economic returns is a considerably more complex matter than the debate about vocational education suggests. Vocationalism pervades the educational system and, as we have suggested, it affects all aspects of schooling. Poor teaching and dreary subject matter appear too often in academic and vocational courses. Whether the curriculum and teaching are rigorous and attractive is of concern wherever they occur. Working hard is an important value in the shop and in the classroom. Indeed, one of the great frustrations with the debate between academic and vocational instruction is the unwillingness to say up front that serious learning in the shop and in the classroom requires hard work. The debate about vocational education is not really about education for work. Rather, it is about the tendency of school programs to perpetuate social class, racial, and gender inequalities and about the tendency of vocational programs to demand less critical reasoning and fewer literacy skills than students have a right to expect. There is no reason why education that is directed at getting a job should do these things, but the fact is that, as currently practiced, it too often does. By funneling students into ability groups and vocational tracks on the basis of presumed capacities to learn and projected occupational roles, we have systematically denied these students access to knowledge and skills essential to their full development as persons, as citizens, and, paradoxically, as workers.

The problem of tracking does not rest simply with the vocational versus the academic tracks. Forgotten in many discussions are the large numbers of students in the third track, the general program. Prepared neither academically nor vocationally, these students are the real losers in the educational system. They are usually taught by the least experienced teachers, given the least interesting course materials, and assumed to perform only at minimal levels. General programs provide few if any learning benefits. Their chief function seems to be to keep youths off the streets; with absenteeism now rampant, they fail even to accomplish this.

In practice, then, much of the tracking currently practiced in schools does not enhance learning. Grouping students is primarily a pedagogical convenience for teachers who believe that this sorting process eases the conditions of teaching. Most tracking is thus a confession of pedagogical failure. But to students it is more than that; all too often, it confirms their own failure to learn in school. Students believe in the labels they have been assigned, and they lose any ambition to achieve beyond these externally imposed categories. Many teachers have had the experience, for instance, of giving students in a lower-track class materials used in a higher-track class, only to find that when the lower-track students discover this, they complain that the teacher is being unfair and expecting far too much of them.

The disinclination to demand much of students in lower-track classes is a denial of the most fundamental aim of the educational system – to develop the capacities of all students. The lower-track students' perception that too much is being asked of them is the most powerful manifestation of the corrosive effects of our tracking practices. We frequently assume that some students are stupid; some students frequently assume much the same thing. The cycle is vicious, and at times seems almost impossible to crack, as countless teachers who have tried have discovered.

The central question is not whether to group students, but how

59

to group them. The practical and pedagogical problem is how to group so that all can learn more. Under the guise of enhancing education, our present tracking system does not do everything possible to enhance learning. It does not do this even for many of those at the top of the system. Instead, it tends to exacerbate inequalities of race and class, and often leads girls and boys into stereotyped programs. Most of all, it leads us to ask much less of students than they deserve. In the process, we limit their options and discourage their willingness to learn.

EDUCATION AND CITIZENSHIP

The belief that a democratic society depends upon an informed and active citizenry has been an essential rationale for the spread of public schooling in America. To the extent that citizens were believed to be equal, the public schools had to concern themselves with equality. To the extent that citizens had to be informed, the public schools had to concern themselves with knowledge.

John Dewey made this point as forcefully as any American. The intimate connection between democracy and education, he wrote in 1916, required that intellectual opportunities be accessible to all on equitable and easy terms. A society that was free, that was "full of channels for the distribution of a change occurring anywhere must see to it that its members are educated to personal initiative and adaptability," Dewey argued, "otherwise, they will be overwhelmed by the changes in which they are caught and whose significance or connections they do not perceive."[12] That was the gravest risk to democracy. Without access to knowledge, citizens would become overwhelmed and withdraw from the responsibilities of citizenship. And with that withdrawal, democracy would be lost.

Dewey's commitment to an educational system that extended everyone's capacity for and commitment to citizenship had been echoed earlier. It was part of Thomas Jefferson's "crusade against ignorance" and was fundamental to the nineteenth-century working men's parties' agitation for expanded public schooling and the commitment of blacks to integrated schools. Democratic citizenship requires the sensitivities and sensibilities to assess, weigh, analyze, and reach conclusions about public and private issues and to act on them. The educational system's obligation is to provide youths with the knowledge, attitudes, and skills that will lead to their full participation in democratic life, from making a living to exercising their rights and duties as parents, individuals, and citizens. To accomplish that task requires an education that enhances literacy, critical thinking, and imagination. Each step we fall short devalues our students and our democratic life.

There is a dangerous and inegalitarian tendency to believe that full citizen participation is not desirable in a democracy, that it is better for officials to make as many decisions as possible and to allow special interest groups and paid lobbyists to influence decision making. Often this argument is based on the view that today's technological complexities are beyond the capacities of most citizens, and therefore, they should not participate in social decision making. Unfortunately, in recent years, such views appear to have gained influence. Fewer Americans seem to take the political process seriously. Among those citizens with less income and less education, the lack of participation is staggering. At the minimal level of casting a vote, we live in a democracy in which large numbers of citizens refuse to participate as citizens.

Schooling is neither the cause nor the cure for this failure of citizenship. Knowledge, literacy, critical thinking, and imaginative expression will not necessarily guarantee that citizens will either participate or make socially desirable choices – by whatever definition of desirable we as a society reach. Still, schools must, as one of their fundamental obligations, take democratic values seriously and be committed, in their curriculum and their practices, to the knowledge, attitudes, and skills that lead to effective and involved citizenship. This places educators in a simultaneous struggle for equality and excellence. Equality is the essential condition of democratic citizenship. Excellence is the necessary condition for making that citizenship meaningful.

4

LEARNING AND EXCELLENCE

D ISCUSSIONS of education are filled with beguiling simplicities. There are, after all, things to be learned; there are the
givens of a discipline or a subject: the curriculum. Tests can be created to measure what is learned and how well it is learned. And once
we know what should be learned and can measure the amount of
learning, then surely we can determine the best way to teach it.

Such simplicities underlie many of the current complaints about
the schools. Academic standards have deteriorated, students are not
working hard enough, teachers are insufficiently accountable. The
remedies then follow: Increase academic requirements for graduation, test students more frequently, lengthen the school day and the
school year. The complaints and the remedies are not necessarily
invalid, but they are oversimplifications.

Consider the following, drawn from polls that ask Americans what
they want from their schools.

(1) Discipline is the most serious problem facing the schools. By discipline, the public seems to mean that students obey the rules and
show respect for authority.

(2) The curriculum should emphasize the basics, particularly mathematics, English grammar and writing, civics/government, U.S.
history, science, and geography, and should contain more practical instruction and more vocational education. These should be
taught so that academic standards are raised, more work done in
school, and more homework required.

(3) Teachers should be well qualified. This seems to mean that they
should be required to pass state board examinations before they
are hired and should be regularly tested thereafter.

(4) The most important reasons for staying in school are better job
opportunities and higher income.

(5) More conferences on the progress of students should be held between teachers and parents. Courses on how to be better parents

should be organized: what to do about drugs, smoking, and alcohol use; how to develop good work habits; how to encourage reading; how to increase interest in school and school subjects; how to help the child organize homework; how to improve the child's school behavior; how to deal with the child's emotional problems.[1]

The overall desire is for greater certainty, higher standards, and schooling that pays off. The sense that students are not learning enough and that teachers are not teaching enough of the basics of subject matter and the importance of the work ethic is a historically persistent and valid concern. Given the anxiety over what happens in schools and the feeling that many young people do not work hard enough, asking for greater certainty, higher standards, and better communication is eminently reasonable.

LITERACY AND EXCELLENCE

But these concerns do not readily translate into effective educational solutions. Simplicities do not remedy complex and deeply embedded problems. The number of people in the United States who lack basic literacy, for example, is staggering. An estimated 25 million people do not possess the skills deemed necessary to function and to participate in society. One person in five in the United States is unable to read and write at a level needed to handle many of the demands of daily living. This functionally illiterate group is overrepresented by the poor and nonwhites. Fifty-six percent of Hispanics and 44% of blacks are estimated to be functionally illiterate; 40% of those with incomes below $5,000 cannot read, compared to only 8% of those with incomes above $15,000.[2]

Much of the public debate over literacy has focused on *basic skills,* which are taken to be an amalgam of reading, writing, and computing. People are thought to be literate if they can fill out forms and read labels, write complete sentences, and do simple arithmetic. These are important and necessary skills. It is to the shame of our society, and not simply of our educational system, that all too many of our youths and adults lack them. But thinking of literacy solely in terms of basic skills is limiting. It leads us to oversimplify complex learning issues, to legislate mandates requiring that everyone, for example, learn to read, and to elaborate programs to test whether the goal has been reached. Most of all, it reinforces the tendency to view literacy and learning as broad conditions that encompass a narrow range of behavior. Such a view of literacy constricts and distorts what we ought to expect from the schools.

Literacy is a complicated and many-faceted phenomenon; it is a developmental process, not a finished product. There are few definitive answers to the questions we regularly ask: Are the young more functionally illiterate today than yesterday? What does it mean for Americans to be scientifically literate or computer literate? The definitions of literacy will always be controversial. They may range from static descriptions like "capable of reading at a fifth-grade level" to more global notions of high standards of rational thinking and scientific and aesthetic comprehension.

What we mean by literacy ought to involve a stress on the possession of analytic skills and the capacity to act using these skills. The definition needs to be flexible enough to make the particular skills needed at any time modifiable and adaptable to changing historical, social, and technological circumstances. Patricia Albjerg Graham offers one such definition, calling literacy the ability "to read, to communicate, to compute, to make judgements and to take actions resulting from them."[3] But even this goal of achieving literacy is not enough. Students need to know how to go about learning; they need to be empowered in a plurality of ways to enhance their understanding and communicate it to others. Literacy then becomes the basis for learning, and can be enlarging and facilitative rather than deterministic and limiting. Such a view of literacy and learning contains a prospect of human potential rather than human limitations. It holds out standards of excellence all too often absent from debates about "basic skills."

An expanded and fluid definition of learning may seem quixotic to advocate when the American public seems almost despairing of achieving adequate and universal forms of literacy in the basic sense of reading, writing, and computing. It has a flair of unreality given the dismal conditions of life and learning in too many schools, where even to get youths to attend daily has become a chronic problem, where teachers have lost traditional authority, and where incessant budget crises threaten to overwhelm all. But an expansive notion of learning is quixotic only if we continue to think of basic skills as somehow divorced from learning as a process of engagement, only if we hold to a view that one first learns basic skills and then uses those skills productively and imaginatively.

The divorce of basic skills from creative thinking and imagination tends to treat schools as minimalist institutions, as places where everyone learns a little and only a few learn a lot. This is contrary to democratic citizenship; the divorce even limits the likelihood of achieving the basic skills. The tendency to divide the process of learning into hierarchical steps and then to treat the learning of basic skills as something that precedes the use of those skills in creative and active ways undermines students' motivation to learn them, as well as teachers' willingness, and certainly their creativity, to teach them. It further defers the gratification that ought to come with learning, for the skills are rarely intrinsically rewarding. For most students, rewards and further motivation come from how they use the skills in the pursuit of knowledge and the development of intellectual, social, and emotional capacities. Treating basic skills as a separate task of schooling subordinates and thus diminishes the range of human knowledge. Aesthetics, emotions, and symbolic expression all become something we do or have, if at all, after we learn to read, write, and compute – a dreary vision that is fundamentally at odds with involving the learner in active interaction with the world. As Mark Twain once suggested, the person who does not read good books has little advantage over the person who cannot read them. A notion of literacy that fixes on but is not equally committed to inspiring in all students the desire and capacity to learn expansively falls considerably short of what we consider schooling to be.

Schools, then, ought to be devoted to teaching students what John Passmore calls *open capacities,* that is, capacities that lead beyond themselves and that open the way to new areas of learning, or, in Jerome Bruner's terms, knowing how to go beyond the information given.[4] That means cultivating attitudes toward learning such that students will *want* to read intelligently, or solve practical and abstract scientific and mathematical problems in whatever shape or form they find them, or seek to participate in and understand music and art as integral to their lives.

Mark Twain, in describing how he became a master riverboat pilot in *Life on the Mississippi* (1883), gave us a vision of learning that incorporates basic skills and the capacity and commitment to go beyond them. Twain's getting to know the river, Joseph Featherstone tells us, is a classic American expression of a metaphor for learning. Twain learns how to navigate the river at a young age. He learns every shoal, snag, and sandbar. These are the basic skills. But no sooner has he memorized their locations and peculiarities than he has to

66

modify or forget them, and learn other spots, for the river never stops changing its course. Twain must simultaneously remember the reality of what existed in the river and imagine how different forces and conditions are likely to change it. He can never know the river completely or certainly; knowledge about the river is always provisional. The point can be generalized: As in Twain's education as a riverboat pilot, action and understanding depend on mastered skills and memory. Yet knowledge is fluid, not solid; understanding is an ongoing process, never ceasing, never absolute. In the process of learning, we, like Twain, continually remake our education, ourselves, and our ways of coping with and understanding the world.[5]

Twain's metaphor offers us a far more complicated but richer vision of learning than the traditional approach of most classes, in which learning is perceived as the transfer of material from teacher to students, and in which knowledge is sharply defined, highly structured, even considered permanent. In such classes, once one has this knowledge, it does not go away; it is quite specific and easily measured. In short, one can either read, write, and compute, or one can't.

In Twain's vision, on the other hand, learning involves these basic skills and competencies, but it also evolves from them. As Dewey taught us, experience is inextricably involved in any education. What one learns beyond the basic skills is hard to measure; it is constantly shifting and being transformed. No single test can measure all of its various dimensions. What one knows must be manifested time and again, adjusted to new situations, criticized, evaluated, and expanded upon. That vision of learning, difficult to implement as it is, should be central to schooling. Instead, it is uncommon. The metaphor of knowing the river rarely intrudes into the curricular guides, the lists of courses, the tests, or the teaching practices of most schools. It is not one with which the public or educators are comfortable. Instead, questions about learning are packaged into curricular and pedagogical compartments: what courses should be required; at what grade level should biology be introduced; how much homework should students do; should teachers lecture or discuss; what kinds of tests should be used? These questions are necessary; it is, after all, difficult to talk about schools without referring to what is being taught and how the material is being presented. To survive in classrooms, teachers must have answers to these questions, and the public has a right to know what they are. But discussions of learning that focus exclusively on such questions are limiting. By preventing us from asking prior and harder questions about what we think knowledge is and what the process of learning involves, they keep us from reaching for significantly better schools and a significantly more empowering conception of learning.

We rarely ask the difficult questions, in part because many educators and the public at large perceive them to be arcane, abstract, and irrelevant. Consequently, almost all of our educational decisions are short-term, open to the fashionable swings of educational fads. We thus move, barely noticing the cyclical nature of the process, from emphasizing the "new" curricula for the best students in the 1950s, to compensatory education in the 1960s, to basic skills in the 1970s, and undoubtedly to the "new" new curricula in the 1980s. The swings are disheartening, not because change is bad but because the changes so often reflect a conception of education that is narrow and limiting. It does not incorporate an expansive view of what learning is and what it can aspire to be.

Taking this larger view would lead schools to consider much more seriously than ever before the development of imaginative expression and critical thinking as educational aims. Learning involves seeing other points of view; understanding, even celebrating, differences; being able to see through stereotypes; being able to transcend custom where it is appropriate, or to support it and its meanings when that is appropriate. Being an active learner, like being an active citizen, requires a flexible intelligence and a mind free, as Matthew Arnold said, of stock notions and habits. The key to flexible intelligence is imaginative and critical thinking.

Imaginative expression is frequently associated with playing rather than working, with imprecision and randomness rather than substance and specificity. Students are supposed to be at work, their minds coming to grips with the *reality principle,* to use Freud's term, rather than dallying with the *pleasure principle.* Given the stern necessity of justifying education in terms of its vocational ends and payoff, there is little utility seen in the development of imaginative expression. Imaginative expression in education has also been ill served by some of its proponents, who often lump it under a generalized "creativity" in which we allow children to "express themselves" in a kind of free-form emoting devoid of knowledge, technique, discipline, or purpose.

Yet imaginative expression should inform almost all human activity. It should not be confined, as its detractors and, all too frequently,

68

its supporters claim, to art or other expressive forms of communication. Nor is it something that is accomplished without knowledge and skills. Imagination infuses the best science as well as the best literature. Indeed, "The generative act in science," the biologist P. B. Medawar tells us, "is imaginative guesswork."[6] Imagination, however, does not float free of knowledge; it is not to be confused with "how I feel" or "how I express myself." Rather, it represents the opposite of "behaving in a routine fashion." It means going beyond everyday observations, everyday experiences, and everyday inferences. Like the capacity for critical thinking, imagination makes it possible to see the world differently, to see possibilities and to "promote a feeling for alternatives."[7]

In cultivating imaginative behavior, teachers are not simply drawing out a capacity inherent in students that needs only to be released, a view held by many child-centered advocates of learning. The cultivation of imaginative behavior requires careful, thoughtful, and disciplined guidance – teaching in the best sense of the word. This teaching is not to be confused with just letting the student's imagination run free, unshackled by the constraints of standards, institutions, or knowledge. We do not "beat the imagination" out of students, although we often so trivialize learning and bore them that their imaginative thinking usually involves ways of getting out of school and its requirements, or is limited to cafeteria escapades or antisocial activities. Like learning itself, imaginative behavior has a multiplicity of dimensions and takes many forms. One person who is particularly adept at human movement may engage in sports or dance with imaginative movements and skills. Another may find verbal skills the basis of imaginative behavior. People may be imaginative in one way, unimaginative in another. The key – and it is central to our view of literacy and excellence – is to stimulate, guide, and expand the dimensions of imaginative expression in all students.

How to do this is much of what teaching is (or ought to be) about. Imaginativeness is encouraged whenever the student can be introduced to what Passmore calls *possible worlds,* and whenever a teacher can break down the student's conviction that the world must be seen in one particular manner, and only one. Urging different perspectives on students opens up the possibility that they can value their own experiences and insights and apply them to what they are learning. It allows them simultaneously to get outside their own world, to be exposed to new and varied ways of thinking about and representing the world, and gives them the opportunity to test their thinking against other perspectives. Motivating imaginative thinking and expression thus involves integrating the security of what students already know with the challenge and the anxiety of what they do not know. The tension is not easy to maintain, but it is hard to believe that without it we can ever get students to think and behave imaginatively.

Like imagination, critical thinking is a perspective, a way of seeking connections and meanings beyond the routine and commonplace. It is not, as is commonly misperceived, the same as being "opposed" to everything. This confuses criticizing with thinking rationally. People who think critically draw upon a body of knowledge and a set of habits and attitudes in order to probe, analyze, or solve a troublesome issue. They place special emphasis on problems that do not have clear answers or that are matters of controversy. A teacher develops students' ability to think critically by challenging them to think within a discipline of knowledge, by encouraging them to evaluate the information they have learned, and by asking them to observe the limits of what they understand. Critical thinking, like imaginative thinking, is not generated in a vacuum. Mastery of knowledge and information is essential; students need something substantial to think about. But critical thinking goes beyond merely acquiring knowledge and information. It involves an understanding of the nature of that knowledge and information, and of the unavoidable biases that are a part of knowledge. It means recognizing the limits to certainty or completeness of knowledge, the limits, for example, imposed on scientific knowledge by the problem raised, by the data sought and used, or by the method of interpreting the data. Or it means understanding "interpretation" in history, literature, or other subjects as an activity involving critical thinking and imagination.

Teaching for critical thinking requires going beyond the all too common notion of "covering the curriculum." Teachers who set out to teach their students to think critically will find their task difficult. There are no ready-made teaching methods. They will encounter resistance from students, principals, and parents. They will have to compete with the pressure of all the other activities of school life. But, as Passmore notes, a teacher who gives up teaching students how to think critically, or doesn't even begin to try, and "salves his conscience by training them in skills . . . should at least be clear about what he is doing, and even more important, what he is *not* doing."[8]

Developing the capacity for critical thinking is important for deciding and choosing what is baseless fabric, for separating the trivial from the serious, the meaningful from the insubstantial. Throughout their lives, students will be surrounded by enticements from all manner of persons; they will be beset by fads, trivialities, and cultists of every stripe promising an elixir or salvation for each and every irritant or tribulation. They will also be exposed to the demands of citizenship in a democratic society. Technological complexity, the interrelation and confusion of political, scientific, social, and economic problems, the fluctuation and divergence of values between various groups, and a host of other uncertainties strain our capacities to know and fulfill obligations, to decide and act in our own and the public good. To act in an informed, responsible, and compassionate way requires the ability to think clearly and critically about issues, to think through the implications of actions, to persuade others. Without these abilities, the motions of citizenship can be easily reduced to empty gestures or rhetorical flourishes. The capacity for critical thinking offers no certainties, no promise of the good, no right decisions. It does, however, permit free choices informed by intelligence, choices that affirm human will and individual dignity.

Imaginative expression and critical thinking are central to any definition of excellence in education. They are necessary if we are to be citizens who take responsibility for our own thinking and actions, and who engage in learning activities beyond formal schooling. Without deliberate attention to the process of learning how to think, the ideal of learning as a process of growth cannot be realized. In that failure, the aim of active and thoughtful citizenship will be lost.

Redirecting schools so that they emphasize learning to think and learning to learn requires us to pay greater attention to the organization of environments for learning. It means attracting and educating people who can be responsible, sympathetic, and demanding teachers. It means making greater efforts to establish outstanding curricula, organized sequences of knowledge that challenge students to learn. The commitment to excellence requires cutting through the custodial function of schooling, which puts students in a temporary holding pattern on the way to adulthood and makes them assume a relatively passive role: always in preparation for action but rarely acting. Learning to think and to learn requires that we understand literacy to be an expansive, even grandiose concept that involves imagination and thinking as integral to what are commonly thought of as basic skills. It asks that students gradually take more responsibility for their own capacities and goals for learning. And it recognizes that self-directed learning and thinking requires teachers who are themselves committed to self-initiated and self-directed learning.

KNOWING AND LEARNING

Learning is a complex activity that varies from person to person. In schools, we tend to oversimplify learning by breaking it down into discrete subjects and allotted time sequences. When the bell rings, science ends and English begins. Sometimes learning is divided into something called *content* or *subject matter* – for instance, the laws of Euclidian geometry or the dates of American history. Sometimes learning is called *process,* the ways information is shared, informally in classroom seminars or through lectures. Teachers often dispute whether they should place more emphasis on content or process. In the elementary schools, teachers emphasize teaching the child rather than the subject; they claim that the process of learning matters most. In the high schools, teachers tend to stress subject matter.

There are still other dichotomies. In the recent past, physical dichotomies were drawn between the right and left hemispheric functions of the brain – the right hemisphere controlling analysis, reason, calculation, explicit description, and the logical functions; the left hemisphere controlling synthesis, recognition of patterns, emotions, and intuitions. Taken at its most extreme, educators would construct curricula and tests that teach and evaluate either the right or the left side of the brain.

The distinctions have some merit, especially in helping us see that learning and teaching involve choices in what is emphasized. But when taken too seriously or when pushed to extremes, the dichotomies are misleading. Take, for example, the dichotomy between objective and subjective knowledge. To have to choose between being objective and being subjective constricts learning. To emphasize only the subjective view of knowledge is constricting inasmuch as it leads students to convert the reasonable view that "everyone is entitled to his or her opinion" into the belief that "everyone's opinion is equally right," thereby denying that there are any definable, objective canons of logic, analysis, or reason. As often noted in classroom discussions in the late 1960s and early 1970s, the treatment of knowledge as subjective leads to an extraordinary personalism and to antiscientific and antirational approaches to issues of thinking and learning. If, in contrast, knowledge is viewed as totally objective, and is discovered and known only through rational processes, our emotions and intuitions about knowledge are considered irrelevant at best and a hindrance to learning at worst. In schools, such assumptions almost always lead to "objective" tests, to drill, and to an emphasis on the regurgitation of facts, as if facts exist outside of their social context. "Fact finding," as Suzanne Langer once pointed out, unfortunately becomes our "common sense."[9]

We cannot, nor do we want to, eliminate either subjective or objective knowledge from the process of learning. Within schools, learning is an interaction between teacher and students in a social setting. Because the curriculum itself is a mixture of facts and values, the beliefs and feelings of teachers and students matter a great deal. What teachers actually teach is shaped by their knowledge, by their habits of thought, by their language, by their feelings, and by the culture and power structures of the school. The curriculum they teach is a product of their own experience. The perceptions of teachers and of students, too, shape the realities of learning as much as the textbooks, lesson plans, or examinations.[10] In effect, the teacher, the students, and the various forms of knowledge are, as Michael Oakeshott has observed, "voices in a conversation, a conversation to which they each contribute in a distinctive way."[11]

This notion of a conversation fuses our ideas of learning and citizenship. The conversation is both learning and how we go about learning. It is important because it leads to individual growth and social empowerment through the directed growth of attitudes, skills, and knowledge. The conversation involves critical, imaginative, and reflective thinking; it involves action and testing of knowledge and skills with others and in the world. It both enriches and empowers individuals and groups. It leads students and teachers into possible worlds, to alternative views, and into a plurality of ways of understanding and making meaning.

We can illustrate what this conversation might be like by thinking about the relationships among aesthetics, emotions, and experience and by assessing what we can expect from scientific literacy. Educators are uncomfortable with diverse forms of representing meaning, particularly if the meaning is not accessible through reading, writing or calculating. In schools, most approaches to aesthetics take the form of art and music classes, which often have to be justified on the grounds that they contribute to the basics of reading, writing, and calculating, an argument that few people believe. Often the arts are considered frills that, depending upon the state of the budget, we can or cannot afford. The perception that the arts are frills is pretty accurate, at least in terms of who takes art and music courses in high school – by all estimates a dismally small proportion of those who graduate.

In itself, that is an unfortunate omission from the lives of students, an indictment of our narrow and partial view of how we learn and know, and a statement that few believe that art and music are sufficiently well taught to attract youths, or that they are worth knowing at all. Yet a rich – and unfortunately ignored – tradition of thought exists that amplifies the importance of aesthetic forms of representing and knowing the world.[12] We should have schools that seek to enlarge students' sense of aesthetics, not by telling them what is beautiful, but by engaging them in creating and thinking about beauty. But we also should value aesthetic education because of the role that emotions and senses play in thinking, and because thinking aesthetically is as demanding and important to students' lives as thinking scientifically, quantitatively, or historically. The tendency in schools and elsewhere to segregate aesthetics and cognition, emotion and knowledge, fails to enrich our understanding of how different modes of learning interact. These limited views of the imperatives of learning, and of our capacities for useful and vital learning, dominate school curricula and teaching. Fluidity of learning in different modes is rejected for spurious certainties about facts and skills; atomized subjects replace holistic learning. The view that thinking in the arts is purely subjective – and hence less important – ignores the cognitive dimensions of thinking aesthetically.

We too often assume that whereas emotion and the senses are important to aesthetics, cognition is supposed to deal with knowing and not with emotion. But, as Nelson Goodman notes, "emotions function cognitively not as separate items but in combination with one another and with other means of knowing. Perception, conception, and feeling intermingle and interact." Or, as Jerome Bruner found when he studied the learning and thinking of mathematics, "it was soon clear that the heart of mathematical learning was tipped well to the left," toward intuition and emotion.[13] The notion that thinking in the arts, or in other modes of making meaning, is purely subjective ignores the cognitive dimensions of thinking aesthetically. The notion that scientific thinking is pure, rational, and detached from human passions and weaknesses is supported by an untenable view of objectivity that seeks at all costs, in Michael Polanyi's words, to eliminate from science "passionate, personal, human appraisals of theories."[14]

Even scientists have deprecated the imagination, wrongly supposing that the so-called experimental method is somehow opposed to it. But science, at its core, is an imaginative experience. As Passmore puts it: "Compared with theoretical physics, *Alice in Wonderland* is a naturalistic novel."[15] Few subjects are as ready-made as science to stimulate imaginative and critical thinking; few subjects are so important in the everyday, practical sphere of our lives or in our larger understanding of the world. Perhaps no other subject or its mode of thinking so touches our lives. From the threat of nuclear annihilation to food additives to miracle medical practices, we are immersed in a flood of science and its technological extensions. Without a basic scientific literacy, ordinary citizens will be totally disenfranchised from the mode of thinking and understanding that is characteristic of our times. The simple truth is that in the late twentieth century, no education can be called excellent that does not include scientific literacy of the broadest kind.

Scientific literacy means knowing some scientific constructs; understanding and being able to practice the processes and norms of science; and being aware of the impact of science and technology on society. No one can know all science; it is possible, however, to know some of the major scientific ideas. Understanding the processes or norms of scientific work involves, at the least, knowing how theories are formed, tested, validated, and provisionally accepted; how to observe and infer; how to recognize that science is a process of successive approximation; and how to encourage more general attitudes (essential to science, but not necessarily confined to it) such as open-mindedness, intellectual integrity, and a willingness to test opinions and beliefs. To be aware of the impact of science and technology means to understand the interactions between science and society in their moral, ethical, and sociological dimensions.[16] Further, it means recognizing that science is an intellectual and social construct deeply rooted in the ethos and historical development of any culture or civilization. Imaginative and critical expression of science comes from this basic literacy. It does not spring from science as readily as Archimedes from his bathtub. The "eurekas!" of science, or any other activity, come only after an accumulation of knowledge, discipline, and hard work.

Currently, there is justifiable alarm about the low number of students taking science or mathematics. Approximately 25% of high school graduates take three years of science, 30% three years of math. The same situation exists in colleges and universities. In the last decade, there was a 64% decline in the number of science teachers being prepared. In 1979, the last time a survey was taken, only 7% of all adults were considered scientifically literate; of those who had only graduated from high school, only 2% were considered scientifically literate.[17]

In response to this current alarm, a number of steps have been taken. A majority of states have upgraded high school graduation requirements to include three years of math and science. School systems and schools of education have made efforts to recruit and prepare new science and math teachers. These and other efforts should alleviate some of the worst problems. But they do little to address what, in our view, are the deeper issues of how science is taught and learned. Science is rarely taught imaginatively. What should be one of the most challenging and creative intellectual activities of schools is too often taught by rote: learning principles and applying them by routine and repeatable procedures.

We need to see science as a part of the educational conversation to which Oakeshott refers. The more scientific knowledge is joined to other forms of knowing, the more it is seen as one form of understanding among many, the more it can add to the educative power of that conversation. Science should not displace the arts or the humanities from the curriculum. All are necessary. The habits of thinking, the perspectives, the data, the ways of classification and verification will differ in the various ways of knowing and expressing meaning. Whereas a scientist tends to think of unique entities in general terms, a humanist or artist thinks of and expresses general entities in unique terms. The scientist attempts to tell us what exists in all times and places, those general, verifiable, and repeatable processes of the natural order. A humanist or artist struggles to tell us what it felt like to live in a certain time or place, or what it feels like to be someone else. Each is engaged, from different perspectives and with different results, in passionate appraisals of human meaning.

Integrating scientific and aesthetic understanding is one way that schools can begin to help students think about learning. Consider the following example of the artist Robert Irwin, observing an adolescent working on an old car. In a commonplace activity, the youth engages in what can easily be considered scientific and aesthetic learning:

> Here was this '29 [Roadster], absolutely dismantled . . . and the kid was making decisions about the frame, whether or not he was going to cadplate certain bolts or was going to buff-grind them or was just going to leave them raw, as they were; and he was insulating and soundproofing the doors. All kinds of things that no one would ever know or see unless he was truly a sophisticate in the area. But . . . real aesthetic decisions, truly aesthetic decisions. Here was a fifteen-year-old kid who wouldn't know art from schmark, but you couldn't talk about a more truly aesthetic activity than what he was doing. How should it look? What was the relationship of its machinery to its social significance? . . . . All these things were being weighed in terms of the significance of how the thing should look.[18]

Like Twain's metaphor of learning the river, the passionate participation in the experience of rebuilding a car is an engagement of mind and body with the world, involving the necessary interplay of symbols, emotions, intuition, language, and objectivity. It also involves the practical dimension of making something. It is an engagement that many teachers understand and that the best of them struggle hard to replicate. We see it frequently outside of classrooms, but only rarely within them.

Learning involves recognizing the patterns among the fragments we see and experience. It involves using a variety of means for describing and engaging with the world. To do this, we need to learn ideas, and to learn how to abandon and transform ideas when they no longer suffice. We need to risk developing our powers of mind to lead us, as Bruner said, to "deeper and more gripping and subtler ways of knowing the world and ourselves."[19]

There is little in the ways we traditionally organize the schools, train teachers, evaluate students, or create curricula that impels us toward such a diverse and enriched conception of learning. Almost none of the recent reports and studies of schools suggests that such an approach would be widely applauded or successfully implemented;[20] indeed, many of the trends toward legislated mandates and simplified testing and evaluation procedures point in exactly the opposite direction. And, as we have already observed, the deplorable levels of basic literacy skills and the extreme difficulty schools are already having in commanding educative power – the power to inspire youths to learn in them – makes it hard even to gain an audience for an enlarged and more enriched view of learning.

We expect students to learn in school, but educators and the public too often establish rules, create standardized curricula and standardized tests, and give out diplomas as if learning were smooth and orderly, as if each step could be planned and executed in predictable sequences. But the process of learning is not so smooth. It is intrinsically disorderly; it means unlearning old notions or ideas, adding new knowledge and skills, experimenting, and deriving coherent meaning from fragments. Its symmetry is rarely experienced in the moment. Within classrooms, the process of learning is a day-by-day phenomenon, the result of interactions among teachers, students, and subjects.

Two further examples give a sense of how varied these interactions can be.

> When the dancers are doing complicated, fast-moving combinations across the floor, the teacher singles out Michelle, a pretty petite black girl, whose steps have been tentative and constricted. "That's a good start, but take a chance, a risk. . . . Go for it, Michelle," he bellows. It is a tough challenge as he makes her do it over and over and again. She is awkward, unbalanced, and almost falls several times, but the dance master will not let her stop. As Michelle struggles to master this complicated step in front of her classmates, some watch attentively without laughter or judgment. Others practice on their own around the edges of the floor, waiting their turn. Everyone, including the teacher, exerts great energy and tries very hard.[21]

In another school:

> One day in accounting, I watched a bored boy carefully writing the names of his favorite bands in fancy handwriting on a sheet of notebook paper. "Charlie Daniels Band," he wrote. "Led Zeppelin." He made the letters by moving his blue ballpoint pen back and forth in tight zigzags, so that the result looked slightly out of focus. You could tell by his expression that he was thinking this kind of writing might not look too bad on an album cover. There were boys in my class who filled page after page in their notebooks with the signatures of rock stars, sometimes slanting the letters to the right, sometimes leaning

them back to the left, one time making an A so that it looked like a little star. One boy I knew has a spiral notebook on the cover of which he has written, each in a different hand, the names of his favorite bands. In the middle of the arrangement surrounded by a jagged halo, was the word "Math."[22]

One student is challenged, the other bored. The paradox of schooling is that the same student will often experience both kinds of classes, sometimes in the same day.

Exactly what the student in the dance class learns is hard to know. She certainly learns more than the subject, in this case a dance step. She is also learning about her own capacities and about the commitment it takes to learn. The young boy who dreams of rock stars is not learning accounting, although he is taking the course. It would be easy, yet false, to account for the differences between the learning experiences of these two students by attributing them to "good" or "bad" teaching or "motivated" or "dull" students. The learning experience of each student depends upon his or her own learning capacities and styles, a large range of teaching styles among teachers, the intangibles of learning in a group with the diverse interests of students and teachers, and the inherent interest of the subject or activity. Curiosity, self-esteem, emotional involvement, ambition, and intellectual interest or facility are not parceled out equally to students or to their teachers.

Stretching students' minds and expanding their horizons will not proceed smoothly or predictably. People find complexity, profundity, and beauty in different things. The diverse reasons for, and approaches to, learning increase the difficulties of schooling: The problem of learning in schools lies in melding the varied interests and ways of learning into a commitment to learn.

Debates about learning should begin with Wittgenstein's question: What is it to understand? What does it mean, for example, to understand a foreign language, a work of art, a scientific theory, a nation's history or politics? How do the various ways of understanding differ from one another, and what do they have in common? How can we best learn what we should know?[23] The answers to such questions are not easily reached, nor are they fixed. But those are insufficient reasons for not asking them. Pursuing the answers – tentatively, questioningly, eclectically – may lead us to recognize that it is not necessary for everyone to know or understand something in the same way, and to recognize that we need to measure learning in a variety of ways. It would help if we accept the idea that there are multiple intelligences and that these intelligences are manifest and expressed in different ways.[24] Similarly, there are many ways of achieving excellence. Schooling that bases its approach to teaching and learning on multiple intelligences and encourages a plurality of excellences will be able to provide experiences for all of its students so that, in Thomas Green's words, *"no one* will be good at nothing, and everyone will be excellent at something."[25]

The process of learning, when it is seriously undertaken, is never inconsequential even if its purposes are obscure. Nor is it confined simply to learning a subject, or facts, or skills. It involves these, of course, but its greater potential is that learning involves an individual in making meaning. This meaning cannot be imposed; it takes different forms for different people. Students who learn engage in making meaning for themselves and others that leads to their full human satisfactions, discontents, and responsibilities. How to help and guide students to learn to make that meaning is the central issue for schools.

PART III
LEARNING AND TEACHING

5

COMPUTERS AND LEARNING

NO innovation holds as much promise for achieving equality and excellence in education as microcomputers. In terms of sheer growth, the promise is enormous. In the mid-1980s, more than half of the schools in the United States had at least one computer available for student use. Despite the financial exigencies of school systems and widespread disagreement over actual costs, the trend toward increased use of computers in learning is accelerating. Textbook publishers estimate that within the decade, more than a third of their business will be in computer software. In the Congress and state legislatures, advocates of computer-assisted learning have been calling for "Apple" bills – tax breaks to companies that contribute computers to schools. Major companies like IBM, Digital, and Apple are giving school systems computers and training. A number of colleges and universities such as Carnegie-Mellon University now treat computers as they do books, as a requirement for every student. Harvard University, among others, has signed agreements with companies to make computers available to students at reduced costs. Today it is almost impossible to discuss learning without reference to computers. Computer literacy is the single most talked about item on the educational agenda.

The growth of computer technology is part of Americans' long-standing belief that machines will change their lives. Nineteenth-century Americans approached technology with a mixture of fascination and fear. The machine would transform and improve their world, but it would also wreck and unsettle the natural order of things.[1] Young Henry Adams reflected some of these feelings in his response to the new electric dynamo he first encountered at the Paris Exhibition in 1900. The exhibition's organizers presented the dynamo as the agent of a new world that would lift the burdens of production and bring joy in its wake. To Adams, the dynamo was an "occult mechanism," its silent whirring a sudden irruption of a totally new force into history, with its social and moral effects unknown.[2]

Similar perceptions are apparent today in the way we think about computers. The fascination with the computer, the sense of promise of the new technology, as well as the fears about its use, have led to a plethora of extravagant claims. Terms like *breakthrough* and *revolutionary consequences* abound. Computer enthusiasts claim that computers and artificial intelligence will change the nature of *Homo sapiens* and bring dramatic alterations in how we think. As David Waltz notes, "The idea that the digital computer will someday match or exceed the intellectual abilities of human beings has been put forward repeatedly ever since the computer was invented."[3] It has been said that a person who is not conversant with the computer will be illiterate and incapable of functioning in the twenty-first century. To some, these projections are frightening. They see the computer as the antithesis of humane and creative thought, a technology unresponsive to emotional needs, a straitjacket on artistic and imaginative behavior. In their view, the computer exalts the technical at the expense of the moral, and potentially damns us to a "Big Brother" society.[4]

This apprehension is appropriate. Computers are likely to alter our lives. They are already dramatically affecting the workplace, changing the number and kinds of jobs available. They are affecting our home and our leisure activities. They are modifying the ways we receive and store information and how we define problems and communicate. They may affect the distribution of power and authority.

In education, computers can be especially powerful in aiding students to think about thinking and to act on their thoughts. Learning with computers can involve logically and/or intuitively conceiving of a problem, exploring possible options for solving it, seeing the consequences of selecting one option rather than another, and establishing a line of action to solve the problem. Enabling students to think is the most important contribution that computers can make to learning. But it is not the only benefit. Computers can provide opportunities to learn and practice a particular skill or skills, giving instant feedback on performance to students and teachers. They can aid in teaching skills like typing and editing. They can test students on the existing curriculum. But much more promising, computers can be programmed by the learners, a process that allows them to tell the computer what to do, thereby drawing upon and strengthening their capacities for performing analytic tasks and for critical and imaginative thinking. Computers can be used for simulation and model building such that students can test the consequences of certain assumptions and make judgments about assumed situations.

But these are only potentials. Their fulfillment depends upon how we answer basic questions about computers and learning. These are the same kinds of questions we have posed in the preceding chapters. Who will teach and learn? What should be learned and under what conditions? How should innovations be implemented? How should knowledge be used?

As we have seen, these questions are central to schooling. But the existence of computers raises them as a special case because the consequences of computers in our lives can be momentous. The use of computers in schools is also at a sufficiently early and fluid state that the answers to the questions are not yet predetermined. Patterns have not yet been institutionalized or rigidified. Few in education are sure exactly how they want to use computers; old teaching habits can be rethought, new practices introduced. That, more than anything else, is the promise of computers – a chance to rethink how we learn and teach.[5]

EQUALITY AND ACCESS

The current and anticipated growth of computer-based learning is both impressive and uneven. Unless corrected, the unevenness is likely to exacerbate inequalities in learning and, in so doing, to undermine the quest for excellence. Access to the computer culture is still heavily dependent upon private markets. In contrast to efforts in the 1960s like *Sesame Street,* which tried to spread educational effects equitably, the use of computers in families means that access to the valued skills and knowledge of the computer is sharply class divided. In 1983, only 3% to 5% of the nation's households had computers, and the mean income of those households was over $28,000.

Unfortunately, the same pattern is occurring within the educational system. Well-to-do school districts obtain computers and train teachers to use them long before inner-city and rural districts. More computers are bought by affluent districts where parents demand, and the schools can afford, the best and the latest for their children. More than three-quarters of the nation's largest, wealthiest high schools have computers for educational use compared to less than half of the smaller, poorer high schools. In financially troubled cities like Boston, Cleveland, and Detroit, there is little access to computers in the schools. At the start of the 1982–3 school year in Boston, only 4% of the city's public school students had access to computers. In affluent neighboring Lexington, computers have been available to students since the late 1950s, and a computer literacy course is required for all seventh-grade students.

The contrast is predictable and discouraging, for it reflects basic inequalities in funding. For many school districts, the issue is not whether computers are desirable or whether one software program is preferable to another, but whether they are affordable at all. Decisions about the use of computers in the curriculum become predicated on financial, rather than educational, considerations. Federal and state efforts to equalize funding are essential. Denying school children access to computers on the grounds of poverty undermines, at the start, the computer's potential to enhance learning for all.

Less obvious, but of similar concern, is the tendency for the computer culture to be a male culture. In some cases, the distinctions are explicit: High schools offer word-processing courses in the commercial and business education departments, overwhelmingly subscribed to by girls. Computer programming courses are offered in the mathematics department, overwhelmingly subscribed to by boys. The course locations communicate different understandings of computers and learning. For girls, the computer is the route to the electronic office. It is a new and necessary form of typing. Boys also learn how to type and do word processing on the computer, but for them, access to the computer potentially involves an understanding of how it works. The use of computers in this way reinforces gender-segregated labor markets and exaggerates inequalities of access to different kinds of knowledge. For girls, stereotypically determined access means that it will be extremely difficult to use computers to learn how to learn.

Overcoming gender discrimination in the use of computers will not be easy. Many children's first and, in many cases, most intense contact with computer technology is through video games of war and violence. Leaving aside the desirability of convincing girls that violence is fun, war is typically treated as a male activity. Girls play video games; boys compete on them. Similarly, because many of the most interesting computer programs are oriented toward mathematics and science, the tendency of teachers and parents to treat these subjects as more appropriately male than female means that boys are more readily propelled toward the computer than girls. These issues obviously go beyond the schools, but if computers are to be available to all students, schools will have to pay more attention to the current biases. They must become actively committed to reducing the anxiety many female students manifest in learning mathematics and must be determined to use computers in nonmathematics and nonscience subjects. Both boys and girls must be taught how to program computers; at least, both ought to feel comfortable "playing" on the computer. Anything less converts inequalities of access into inequalities of knowledge.

Finally, if schools are to enhance equality and excellence in learning, they must shift away from the current tendencies to use access to computers as a reward for the gifted student and to grant access to the slower student only for programmed remedial instruction. In all too many schools, fast learners are rewarded with time on the computer, often with considerable freedom to explore its uses. For them, computers become learning machines through which they create and debug programs. Slower learners are either denied access, because they rarely finish their required work with sufficient speed, or are sent to the computer for drill and rote learning tasks. The discrepancy in both access and quality of use further reinforces the inequalities that so often undermine excellence for all students.

In each of these areas – the discrepancy between affluent and poor school districts, between males and females, and between the gifted and the slow student – issues of access and use are critical. Those denied access are denied knowledge. Those discriminated against in the kinds of learning made available to them are denied access to computer literacy. A new kind of tracking system is instituted, one that replicates the inadequacies of the existing system. The issue of access is thus the place to begin, for without serious attempts to address inequalities there, the promise of computers to enhance learning will be undermined. The potential solution becomes a new form of the problem of inequality.

TEACHING MACHINES/LEARNING MACHINES

Computers change the form, scope, speed, and accessibility of information. They make possible new ways of organizing facts; they allow facts to be placed in different combinations to illuminate relationships that might otherwise go unnoticed. But facts and information should not be confused with knowledge and education.[6] In *Hard*

Times, Charles Dickens tried to illuminate these distinctions by giving us Mr. Gradgrind, who saw education as consisting of nothing but the accumulation of facts. "Facts alone are wanted in life," he said. "Plant nothing else, and root out everything else. You can only form the minds of reasoning animals upon facts; nothing else will ever be of any service to them." Gradgrind envisioned a thoroughly information-based society: "We hope to have, before long, a board of fact, composed of commissioners of fact, who will force the people to be a people of fact, and of nothing but fact."[7]

To Mr. Gradgrind, facts constituted the sole truth. Boris Pasternak knew differently: "What is laid down, ordered, factual," he wrote, "is never enough to embrace the whole truth; life always spills over the rim of every cup."[8] This tension between subjective and objective is the essence of learning. The same dilemmas that we posed in Chapter 4 – how to combine subjective and objective learning in schools and how to expand notions of literacy to include imaginative and critical thinking – are raised by the use of computers in learning.

Far too often, Seymour Papert argues, computers are used in schools simply to put children through their paces in standard exercises, drills, and other busy work, providing feedback and dispensing information. Outside of schools, computerized games are sources of entertainment, commanding young people's attention and commandeering their allowances. In both cases, the computer programs the child. Yet, the interactive capabilities of computers, what is called their *holding power,* can be used to stimulate and to structure the thinking of students. The difference between students playing ready-made programs and devising their own has immense implications for education. In the first case, the computer acts as a "teaching machine"; in the second, it becomes a "learning machine."[9]

"Project Logo" is an example of an activity in which students tell the computer what to do.[10] The project creates an environment in which students learn to think in different ways. It is based on a model of learners who think about what to do and request that it be done. When the outcomes are not what the learners expect or wish, they debug – that is, they figure out what is wrong and make the necessary corrections. There is no voice or statement saying that they are wrong. Rather, the images before them do not conform to what they desired. Learners begin to think about their own thinking, becoming, as it were, epistemologists. Over time, they ask the computer to do more, and their greater knowledge and higher expectations lead them to be both more certain and more uncertain of the results. Before a subject is learned and before learners turn to prepackaged software for instruction, they have become well acquainted with the functioning of the computer. They have learned, most importantly, how to use the computer for exploration and new understanding.

Unfortunately, most students' interactions with computers are not of this kind. In most cases, the new technology is simply superimposed on traditional methods of teaching. Computers are used for drill and practice, making them little more than expensive flash cards. The organization of schools makes this likely. Subjects have to be studied; assignments need to be done on time; and teachers find it hard to conceive of learning without an existing textbook. Access to the computer has to be limited – because of costs, numbers, and scheduling, and because access is treated as a special reward. Who has time to let students debug? And what difference does the debugging make if it is not directed toward the existing curriculum?

As school systems and teachers search for ways to incorporate computers into their programs, they tend to turn to prepackaged software. Indeed, the production and distribution of computer software has already become a major growth industry. Specialized software companies are proliferating, seemingly unaffected by either declining school enrollments or budgetary constraints. The most immediate effects of this new competition have been to bring down the cost of computers and to increase the technical sophistication of the software. But the desire for instant marketability has also resulted in software that is low in quality, homogeneous, and unimaginative.

The problems of computer software have been accentuated by the uncertainty many educators feel about the appropriate uses of computers. They are uncertain about whether all, or only some, students should be exposed to computers. They are uncertain about whether students should be closely supervised on the computer or allowed to explore on their own. They are uncertain about the purposes of computer-assisted instruction. They feel a tension between their students' expectations that computers are entertaining and fun and their own concern that the course curriculum be followed. In the absence of any definitive leadership from the educational community in resolving these questions, software producers have taken the initiative in two ways.

First, software producers believe that learning packages must be fun. For students to learn about computers, they assert, the software needs to hold their attention. Fun projects mean that students can be put on computers without having to be constantly overseen. Entertainment values predominate, and computer-assisted learning is treated as a reward for those students who do their school work.

Second, software producers tend to view computer-assisted learning as a supplement to the existing curriculum. Their software packages look as much like standardized subject matter and existing textbooks as possible, sometimes in the form of remedial course work, sometimes as learning programs for advanced students. One publishing company has been explicit about this practice, planning the same format for its software products as exists for its printed curriculum materials, making the two interchangeable.[11] Much software, then, is simply a textbook or workbook placed on the computer.

Software producers are likely to continue taking these approaches until educators demand more educative and intellectually innovative programs. Unless creative software takes advantage of the potential of computers, computers in classrooms will become simply toys, to be put away when teachers don't want their students to play with them. Or computers will be used simply as supplements to or replacements for current textbooks, without any clear advantages other than having students spend time on the computer. If inadequate and boring textbooks are the stuff of computer software, as they all too frequently are, or if computers are used primarily as instruments of drill and practice, then a sophisticated technology is wasted on a task that can be easily accomplished with the traditional use of book and pencil.

The computer culture is still young, the range of options not yet determined. The intense competition in the field provides the opportunity for educators to shape and to choose what materials will be available. If educators decide what they want from computers and how they expect to use them, and if they are willing to think creatively about the learning possibilities inherent in computers, they may be able to help the schools invest productively in new hardware and software.

TEACHERS AND THE NEW TECHNOLOGY

Computers will become learning machines in the schools only if teachers are themselves comfortable and proficient in their use and involved in introducing computers into schools, deciding their appropriate applications, and monitoring the quality of the software used. Teachers cannot participate effectively in such decisions, however, if they are untrained in the use of computers or are fearful of or alienated from them. We cannot afford to ignore just how unfamiliar most teachers are with the new technology, nor the educational consequences that arise from that unfamiliarity. Some of the problems are generational: Many young people are more comfortable with and more knowledgeable about computers than adults. Students are more willing to invest their time and energy; they use the language more easily; and they produce results as capably as adults. In classrooms where students have experienced computers at home or in other settings, many teachers find themselves especially uncomfortable; many students find computers to be ordinary, like televisions and telephones.

Because of their unfamiliarity with computers, many teachers downplay the role of computers or limit their use to mundane tasks. The software currently being produced furthers this process by assuming, accurately, that most teachers have little knowledge of how computers operate. Like the programmed textbooks produced some years ago, the strategy adopted is to design software that is teacher-proof. One example is the DISTAR program created to teach English language skills to the "culturally disadvantaged." The program is organized so that students cannot modify the course format and teachers need not worry that anything but the right answer will be accepted. As two analysts of the program report, "The teacher's manual for DISTAR describes one, and only one, method of conveying each lesson or rote drill. Any deviation from the prescribed words is forbidden."[12]

Although everyone seems to win in such a process – the computer people get computer-assisted learning into classrooms, students get to work on the computer, and teachers get their standard lessons taught – in fact the losses are enormous. The process is arrogant in its disdain for what teachers can learn and accomplish. Teachers are treated as if they are incapable or irrelevant. Students are given little or no opportunity to explore new areas of computer use. And, in the end, these curricula generally get put aside. They seem to satisfy no one. Trying to separate computer-assisted learning from teachers makes no sense at all.

Computers can be employed in ways that promote students' learning. Teachers can utilize the holding power of the computer to stimulate students' thinking about their own thinking. To do so, teachers must have the programming skills necessary to develop software appropriate to their students, to their subject matter, and to the available hardware. Above all, teachers need to feel comfortable with computers, both so that they can use computers to enhance their teaching and so that they will be willing to let their students experiment with them. Not every teacher has to be a computer expert or know more than every student. Obviously, teachers will differ in their view and treatment of computers. But few teachers will allow their students to explore the computer's potential or provide leadership in that exploration unless they themselves are comfortable or skillful on the computer. At a minimum, it makes sense for teachers to have some programming skills and to know where to get help with more advanced computerized learning.

Computers will not replace teachers any more than pencils or slide rules have done. In fact, as an NEA survey affirms, many teachers are willing to make greater use of computers and are interested in acquiring new computer skills.[13] At a simple level, many teachers facing enormous work loads can get valuable assistance from computers; many routine tasks — keeping records and track of individual instruction programs and creating worksheets, for example — can be handled quickly and efficiently by computers. But, more important, teachers will be less effective as teachers if, out of fear or ignorance, they treat computers only as threatening devices to be resisted at all costs.

School systems will thus have to make greater and more direct efforts to aid teachers in developing teaching strategies appropriate to the new technology. They will need outside help and resources to do this. The assumption that teachers do not have to have special knowledge to make effective use of computers or that software programs are available that do not require teachers will doom computer use to the mundane or to total neglect. Computers offer tremendous opportunities for learning, but they are not educational elixirs. They will not solve all or even the majority of educational problems. With the active involvement of teachers and the encouragement for them to experiment, however, computers can greatly enhance students' creative thinking and imagination.

MEDIATING VALUES IN A COMPUTERIZED SOCIETY

Teachers must do more than simply teach students computer skills. They must help students grapple with what Marshall McLuhan called the *electronic surround*. In so doing, they can help students see that computers do not provide "solutions." Teachers can use the issues surrounding computers to do what the best teachers have always done: enhance students' search for meaning and understanding in a chaotic world.

The use of computers raises ethical issues that ought to be addressed as part of learning about computers. If teachers are to help students understand the functions, purposes, and limitations of technology, they themselves will have to avoid getting caught in what William Barrett has called the *illusion of technique*.[14] They should encourage students to address social and political issues: the effects of an increasingly sophisticated "information society" on privacy, the disenfranchisement of those who remain technically ignorant in a technological society, the propensities for control of people through control of information.

Knowledge of the computer is, in essence, knowledge about how to doubt, evaluate, and criticize, as well as use. It is an enlarged notion of common sense. All youths should learn to use computers, to engage in problem solving, and to write programs. That is the technical side of computer literacy. But unless these are taught in a context of social and political issues, they become simply technical skills and do not incorporate critical thinking and imaginative expression.

This enlarged notion of computer literacy parallels our understanding of how to think about literacy more generally. Unless we understand that the hierarchical distinctions among technical skills, programming, creativity, and critical analysis are artificial, we will undermine the potential for all students to work on computers and to think about them. For some students, this will not be an issue. Whatever capacities schools may develop in computers, these students will have far more sophisticated hardware and software at home; they will be fully capable and innovative programmers; and they will be aware of the social impact of computers. (These students can be a valuable resource for teachers to use as aides.) For the vast majority of students — at least at the present time — private markets do not offer the opportunity to become computer literate. Indeed, for most of them, contact with computers outside of the school comes through games in a video arcade. For them, computers are sophisticated toys whose sole immediate function is competitive entertainment tied to names like "Communist Mutants from Space," "Chopper Command," "Megamania," "Lazerblast," "Demon Attack," "Astrowash," and the like.

We need not assume that all of these games stifle intellectual development or orient young people to violent activities. Nevertheless, we ought to be concerned about the values these amusements represent and promote and about the potential effects on young people who are the consumers in a fiercely competitive market. Schools will certainly have to acknowledge the attractiveness of these games – at least to boys, who seem much more prone to play them than girls. Schools will have difficulty serving as an antidote or corrective to the cumulative miseducative effects of the popularized computer culture. But schools can provide students with alternative visions of how to use computers to involve their imaginations and engage them in thinking creatively about problems. School-based computers will not replace video games; they can be used to ask students to think about these games. They can also be used to help students and teachers think about how they think.

Computers ought to sharpen the debate over the purposes of schooling. They are not panaceas either to learning or to the difficult problems our schools face. We need to pose the same kinds of questions about computers that we pose about other parts of the learning and teaching environment: how computers will be used to stimulate imaginative expression and critical thinking; how they will be used to enhance the goals of equality and excellence; how they will be used to get students to think about thinking. With the knowledge and capacity to go beyond facts, beyond the information given, we can begin to approximate a literacy that is expansive and fluid. Without emphasizing how to use information and to what ends, the use of computers can be a numbing intellectual experience. Students will be exposed to information that is categorized, canned, and packaged, with the effect of stopping thinking dead in its tracks.[15]

6

THE PROMISE OF TEACHING

"YOU get worn right down," a teacher in Berkeley said. "You don't get very much support."[1] Fresh faces appear in classrooms with every new school year, new promises, new lives, new needs. The work of teaching proceeds minute by minute, hour by hour, day by day, a slow, steady accretion of facts, skills, techniques, details, the responses sometimes grudging, sometimes enthusiastic, the rewards uncertain. "Teaching is like housework," another teacher said. "It's never noticed until it's not done properly."[2]

Although these teachers undoubtedly speak for many of their peers, no teacher is typical; each survives and flourishes in distinct ways. A small-town elementary school teacher may treat her students as her own. They are members of a community to which she belongs. Often she has grown up either in or near the town. Her anxieties turn on the effects of classroom conditions upon her ability to love and guide her charges. A teacher in a larger urban community questions whether she can do anything to overcome the learning and behavioral problems that confront her. Poverty, unemployment, and racial discrimination set the terms of her interaction with students. She talks openly of their effect on her classrooms. A suburban teacher tries to impart the subject matter of her curriculum to students while meeting the demands of new agendas: drug education, alcohol education, sex education. The new agendas are part of a process whereby schools have become agencies for solving social problems. These become the tasks of schools, and when the problems do not disappear, teachers are seen as having failed to educate their students satisfactorily.

Whatever their setting or their approach to teaching, a large number of teachers are frustrated, feeling the effects of difficult working conditions, public hostility, and public demands. The current agitation to improve the schools is double-edged for teachers. Although it has focused attention on the need for greater commitment to the public schools, it has been almost unremitting in its condemnation of the quality of teachers and teaching. Over the last decade, teachers' salaries have decreased relative to those in other occupations, limiting the appeal of teaching. Since 1970, the scores of prospective teachers on standardized tests have declined precipitously. The best teachers appear to be leaving the classroom in greater numbers than the less adequate. Working conditions in many schools are poor, and worsening. The day of a male English teacher in an urban high school illustrates just how difficult the conditions are. The teacher arrives at school around 8 A.M. and has a thirty-minute preparation period before the students arrive. He teaches five classes of twenty-seven students each and has supervisory obligations during a sixty-minute period. He is not given extra time to eat lunch. At 3 P.M. he leaves. (If he does not, he is breaking the contract. The union in his district insists that teachers not work beyond the end of the school day.) He almost certainly has a second job to go to (or an income-earning spouse). At age sixty-five, his final salary is about that of a beginning city lawyer. In cities like New York, Detroit, San Diego, New Orleans, and St. Louis, conditions are even worse. There, the load is thirty-five pupils per class, not twenty-seven. Although the teachers get a lunch break, they are required to work longer into the afternoon.[3]

Lonely in their work, teachers are expected to keep performing day after day, year after year, with little opportunity for personal or professional renewal and development. Their tasks from year to year are strikingly similar. What is expected of a thirty-year veteran parallels that expected of a novice. Teachers spend almost the whole of their working day in the company of children; their contact with adults is usually fleeting and rarely concerned with professional matters of teaching. The moments away from students are often devoted to conserving energy, to taking deep breaths, or to churning out ditto sheets and lessons for the next day's classes. After a few years of teaching, many teachers complain that what began as a dynamic activity becomes routine. What once was and should remain energizing – the process of inquiry and learning – becomes debilitating. The enthusiasm that once inspired individuals to work with children or teach the subjects they enjoyed becomes alienation. One teacher with ten years of experience describes her frustration: "You have to find ways to make what you do day after day in the classroom new, and you have to get something out of it for yourself. It has to have some personal meaning. But no one cares. There is little support. I often feel – not like an island – but a chunk of land that's been worked away from the mainland and could be overcome by the sea."[4]

Her feelings reveal the sense of isolation that so often affects teachers. They also reflect the impact of the last decade of heightened expectations and denunciations. Teachers have been caught between local demands and federal and state regulations and mandates. Experts from outside the schools have evaluated and criticized teacher performance. The bureaucracy of many schools, the paperwork, the management-by-objectives mentality of many administrators, the demands for teacher accountability, the custodial obligations, the rhetoric of community and parental involvement, even the aspiration to collegial decision making have all deflected teachers from working with their main constituency – the students. Rarely has so little attention been given to how teachers teach and how they manage to teach. The efforts to force teachers to march to a basic skills curriculum, or to challenge their authority to set standards, have further denigrated what teachers do and their legitimacy as professionals. Teachers are condemned for not being self-regulating. They are condemned for not having high standardized test scores. They are held accountable to a public board of education and to a bureaucracy downtown, and their unions' activities in defense of job security and salaries appear to the public as insensitivity to the taxpayers who support them and the students they are supposed to teach. The teachers have become targets; for many critics, they are the cause of the problems. They are caught between being asked to do more and being given less support to do it.

Few people expect teachers to be like Mr. Chips – ever available, always inspiring, committed, wise, personable, and humane. Yet, there is a wistfulness about our image of teachers, a wish that they be like Mr. Chips or, in the female version, the dedicated woman of an earlier generation who saw her teaching as missionary work, who received small economic benefit from it, and who spoke to her students with authority. The image is of the all-powerful teacher, relatively untouched and untainted by organizational and political constraints. She taught a curriculum that did not bend to the whims of political activism. She taught history and literature – not black or women's history or popular culture.

Such views are only partially accurate, more of the oversimplifications and mythologies that mar our understanding of education. They

97

emphasize, in this respect rightly, that teachers are important, indeed crucial, to the educational enterprise. But the idealized portraits, as well as the strident condemnations, are a far cry from helping us understand the realities of teaching and the dilemmas of practice. They impede a full appreciation of just how hard it is to teach well, and how teaching and learning might be improved and sustained.

THE PRACTICE OF TEACHING

Teachers are constrained by the fundamental ambiguities of their craft. They are uncertain that they can make all of their students learn; they are uncertain whether they possess the skills to excite all of their students. Many teachers recognize that teaching is a hit-or-miss affair, that there are no certain scientific methods. Their disappointments are frequent; their doubts that they have done their best are pervasive.[5]

Teachers want to teach and they want their students to learn. They want to have good relationships with their students. Most admit to being frustrated in meeting these expectations, and indeed, the number of discouraged teachers appears to be increasing. They give all sorts of reasons for their frustrations: lack of public support, funding cutbacks, the decline of family discipline (often blamed on divorce and single parents), bureaucratic interference, unsupportive colleagues, an anti-intellectual pop culture. The reasons sometimes come across as rationalizations, as ways of externalizing the problems. But whether these analyses are accurate or not is less important here than the teachers' insistence that, more than anything else, they want the chance to teach well.

Students, in turn, say they are bored with school. They claim that their classrooms are stultifying. Judging by the ways they act outside the classroom, they are right. Little of the life and vitality of the hallways, playground, or nonschool activities appears inside classrooms; teachers teach, and students try to let the teaching intrude as little as possible. Recognizing this fact, some teachers try to innovate and inspire; others are content to keep the boredom from becoming a disciplinary problem. Few, however, dispute the students' claims, although from the teachers' point of view, the problems of student boredom become problems of student motivation.

These are not new issues. Teachers have always wanted to teach, and they have historically expressed frustration over the results of their efforts. In his classic study of teaching, *The Sociology of Teaching* (1932), Willard Waller reported that over time, teachers experienced disillusionment with their occupation. They wanted to escape from the classroom; they lost their enthusiasm and became impassive and inflexible. Other studies similarly suggested that students looked upon schools without much enthusiasm. One New York City high school teacher summarized the results of a 1940 survey by declaring that the students "do not look at school as a place of joy or pleasure. There is no exuberant enthusiasm displayed. . . . The children attend school with consciousness that it will help them out in later life. School is not pleasurable for itself."[6]

The historical continuities indicate that the dilemmas of teaching are not susceptible to easy fixes. They are deeply rooted in the practice of teaching itself. Teachers teach in classrooms with twenty to forty students. They understand that every classroom is composed of students with different needs, desires, abilities, interests, and personalities. They try in myriad ways to respond to each student differently so that each student has a distinctive experience. But they also recognize that every classroom must be organized so that individual energies and differences are bound and integrated into a smoothly functioning whole. Even as they teach an entire class, teachers have to be aware that their students are learning individually. The experience of learning in classrooms is simultaneously common and individual.

Teaching is also complicated by the negotiations of the classroom. Every teacher "bargains" with his or her students. Sometimes the bargains enhance learning: "I will make extra efforts to motivate you if you approach learning with goodwill." Sometimes the bargains corrupt learning: "I won't demand much from you if you behave and do the limited amount of work I assign." Or, because the message from the administration is "we do not want any trouble or complaints," teachers must put much of their efforts into getting along with their students. As Philip Cusick writes in his study of three Michigan high schools, "teachers who hold up a strong academic ideal, who demand homework, quiet, writing skills, who do not give good grades without some effort are more likely to antagonize students and their taxpaying parents, have students avoiding their classes, and have conflicts which wind up in the office."[7] No wonder so many teachers choose to avoid demands on their students. But whatever the result of any particular classroom bargain, the larger point is that there are no bargain-free classrooms.

The ambiguities and the bargaining complicate the practice of teaching. Teachers speak about this in contradictory ways. Some teachers speak as if they could teach their students anything if the circumstances were right; some teachers express doubts that they can teach their students very much at all. Some teachers suggest that if there were no external intrusions, they could teach effectively and students would learn. If principals and bureaucrats would get off their backs or support them in the face of parental complaints, if Christmas and lunch money didn't have to be collected, if parents would properly feed, clothe, and discipline their children, if television and arcade games did not exist, if government regulations were not so intrusive, the worst problems would disappear. Teachers consider a good day one in which the outside world is absent from the classroom, "a day when you can close the doors and do nothing but teach."[8]

At the same time, teachers doubt that they can teach so that every student can learn to the best of his or her ability, even under the most auspicious circumstances. They wonder whether they are doing enough to teach all their students. Teachers express delight when their students tell them they have learned and take their greatest pleasure from individual student gains. But they are often surprised that their teaching has actually caused students to learn, and they are very uncertain that they can reproduce the experience with the next student.

Teachers get their greatest satisfaction from their classroom successes. They want, as Dan Lortie suggests, "to feel they have reached their students – their core rewards are tied to that perception."[9] This does not mean that work conditions and salaries, job security, funding, school–community relations, extracurricular activities, and the rest of the things that occupy teachers' time are unimportant. It does mean, however, that what most teachers are most concerned about is teaching their students, with all of the uncertainty, ambiguities, frustrations, and exhilaration of that experience.

Not all teachers have the same commitment to having their students learn, but for the overwhelming majority, teaching well is their primary goal. For them, a central issue is to motivate every student to want to learn what is being taught. How, they often ask themselves, can they engage students in the time-consuming and some-times painful process of learning? Teachers confront a range of student attitudes from hostile, recalcitrant, and apathetic to enthusiastic and highly motivated. Peer group pressures can as easily coalesce around the former as around the latter. One teacher can find a group or an individual student enthusiastic; another meets apathy from the same group or individual.

To many teachers, student motivation to learn has always been the central issue. But despite the scores of curriculum and pedagogical reform efforts and the plethora of sociological and psychological research reports, this goal remains elusive. What is clear, however, is that exhortation and threats have a limited effect. Threats such as "If you don't learn, you will not be occupationally successful" or "You will not be a good citizen or be able to lead a creative life" tell students that what happens in the classroom is important only because it will affect their future. Making the school important only for reasons other than learning makes it hard to give the school educative power and diminishes its ability to engage young people's curiosity about themselves and their world. Students are concerned about what is right and what is wrong, about how to live, as well as about how to be successful. They are completely engaged in questions of vital importance. Good teaching capitalizes on this interest and motivates learning by acknowledging the legitimacy of the concerns of the young. Good teachers do not romanticize their students' concerns, nor do they use them in order to punish students. They recognize that teaching involves a simultaneous process of reaching out toward students and demanding more of them.

Every teacher knows that the results are not guaranteed. Students must make some commitment to their own learning. It is something they have to choose to do themselves: Learning, knowledge, and skills must be received, taken, and converted into action. This requires hard work, discipline, and commitment. Teachers can only go so far with students who will not make the effort to learn. Most teachers see the task of motivating students as an attempt to convert disinterest into a desire to learn. To motivate students to do that requires both a sympathetic involvement in students' lives and a demand that they learn, the process Lortie describes as teaching "tough" and getting along with students. It means more than telling students to "do this" or "learn that." It means using techniques to provoke, persuade, cajole, and coerce students to learn. Sometimes they will not succeed; some students are beyond the reach of formal education; some are impervious to even the very best teachers. Teachers cannot motivate students, however, if they ask little of them. Minimum expectations too easily become all that is required. Every student has the right to expect that more be asked; every teacher has the obligation to ask for more.

No one method, technique, or approach is the right one. There is no single definition of the good school or teacher. But whatever the variety, great teaching begins with the expectation that students can and should learn. It requires, in addition, caring for students and knowledge of the subject. We are all familiar with teachers who care, whose love of students and subject, dedication and enthusiasm transcend any limitations they may have had. It is amazing how many of those teachers are remembered for the effect they had on us when those who were merely technically proficient recede into the shadows.

Teachers themselves, reflecting on what they find compelling in their teaching role models, say that the quality of caring is as important as skill. They respect and admire other teachers who gain affection and respect from students, who get their students to work, and who are effective in winning student compliance and discipline. They perceive great teaching as a combination of instructional skill and caring. Caring does not necessarily mean merely being warm and friendly; a teacher can care that students learn, or that they feel good about their learning, or that they work hard to achieve their best. In their role models, teachers admire diverse qualities and skills; their comments give a sense of their beliefs: "She was excellent, if you could survive . . . [she was] cynical and sarcastic . . . [gave] clear-cut cold information. She was really good"; "She was peppy and full of fun, we learned, we worked harder than we probably realized we were working but we loved it"; "He was a teacher. It is intangible. He loved his work and spread that love to students."[10]

Caring on its own, however, is insufficient to stimulate high levels of learning. Knowledge of the subject is necessary – the awareness that comes with having mastered a discipline, the satisfaction that comes when this mastery is transmitted to students. Knowing the subject does not guarantee effective teaching, but without it, it is hard to imagine a teacher able to guide his or her students through the myriad ways to explore the subject or willing to let them experiment with different ways of knowing. Indeed, one of the discouraging features of teaching has been the limited knowledge expected of teachers. How that knowledge is best transmitted in ways that tap and extend teachers' desire to teach and students' motivation to learn is a question to which we will return. But recognizing the complexity and ambiguity of teaching and the necessity that teachers be both caring and knowledgeable is an imporant first step in improving practice.

THE PROCESS OF CHANGE

Whether they wish to be or not, teachers are models of thinking; they are images for their students of the potential of the life of the mind. The importance of teachers as learners, or the importance of teachers as models of learning for students, cannot be overemphasized. Unfortunately, what we expect of students we too often deny to teachers: Whereas we ask students to commit themselves to learning, we fail to provide teachers with similar opportunities to learn. If the schools are to be primarily places to learn, then those who teach in them must be engaged in learning. Good teaching is the product of continuous learning. It is incredible to recognize how little attention is given to this simple proposition. The crippling expectation that teachers will be complete professionals at the end of their training or probationary period of teaching neglects entirely the dynamics of teaching as a learning activity. We tend to treat teaching as separate from learning or, when we ask teachers to learn, we neglect to offer them the requisite opportunities and professional incentives. Good teachers are able to open up the play of their minds to their students. They are invaluable models of learning.

Any emphasis on teachers as learners must begin by acknowledging and building upon teachers' experience and expertise. For teachers, the need to have their experiences taken seriously is especially strong because of the pervasive childishness of the settings in which they work and the students with whom they interact. In his study of teacher attitudes and behaviors, Dan Lortie found that teachers often worry aloud that their constant interaction with children might diminish their adulthood or reduce their intellectual capacities. They hunger to spend more time with adults and to be treated like adults. As one said, "If you stay with the students too long, you get to talk like them sometimes. You don't come in contact with too many adults, and your students, you are supposed to talk down to their level so that they can get it." Another commented, "I just think you sort of stagnate in a way. You could stagnate more if you wanted to let it happen, if you did not read, etc., but I would just like to give and take with adults once in a while."[11]

More is required than simply interacting with adults. Those interactions must be based on the content and practice of transmitting knowledge, or gaining new knowledge, and of reconceptualizing what is already known. That means encouraging teachers to reflect on their professional experience. If reflection is extended, pushed, challenged, then new conceptualizations are possible, and teachers can engage in the ongoing process of learning about what and how they teach.

Improvements in teaching, then, must proceed with the active involvement of teachers. But teachers who feel overworked and underappreciated are not likely to assume new roles and responsibilities. Nor are they likely to reinvigorate the education of their students if they themselves are weary, bored, or alienated. Yet, ironically, teachers often suffer most from the process of school reform. New programs increase teachers' burdens and further confuse what is expected of them and their students. New programs often demand of teachers more knowledge and new techniques. They require changes, but rarely give teachers enough time or resources. The reforms require experiments but provide no room for failure.

Reform efforts place teachers in a double bind: Although the reforms may be educationally desirable, they complicate the teaching process. Teachers find it difficult to be enthusiastic about curriculum innovations or the mainstreaming of handicapped students when their classrooms are made more complicated by the changes, when they are condemned for being inflexible, and when they are given little help in making the changes expected of them. Reforms considered educationally enlightened (such as the vogue for "individualized instruction" or the plea to use computers) have not been implemented due to organizational structures over which teachers have little control. But invariably, when the reforms fail, teachers are blamed.

In part, teachers often find themselves in such a bind because the origins of most educational reforms lie outside of schools. Governments, courts, community activists, university-based experts, and school bureaucracies impose the reforms. With few exceptions, teachers are ignored in the process. Some reform initiatives undoubtedly have to come from the outside. It would be hard, for example, to conceive of the equity gains in education made by minorities and women during the last two decades occurring without the civil rights movement and federal action. Heightened national interest and a surge of federal funding fueled the desire to increase equity and promoted curricular and pedagogical experimentation. Capitalizing on these initiatives, many teachers opened their classrooms to new ideas and new approaches.

But these reforms left other teachers alienated and confused. As Harold Howe II has noted, teachers often find themselves "caught in a vast system of regulation, rules, and objectives . . . defined for them by policy requirements concerning disadvantaged students, school desegregation, handicapped children, achievement measures, accountability systems and the like." Even when regulations affect their classrooms only slightly, the sense of being imposed upon is rampant. What begins as attempts to renew education seems too often to teachers like unwarranted attacks on the worth of their work. Little wonder that teachers often circle their wagons and attempt to protect themselves from the intentions of superintendents, professors, curriculum experts, and principals. The reform of education, in which teachers are among the objects to be reformed, leaves many teachers feeling the heavy hand of bureaucracy pressing on the "intricate, complex, and little understood circumstances that comprise the teacher/learner relationship in the classroom."[12]

Heavy-handed, top-down approaches to reform are neither the only way to improve practice nor, as the experiences of the 1950s and 1960s suggest, are they the most effective. Rather, reform needs to begin by recognizing that teaching is an ambiguous and uncertain craft, that teachers teach in the differing environments of a particular school, and that they are isolated in their own classrooms. Efforts to improve teaching and enhance learning have to be based in individual schools and involve collaborative planning. Demands for accountability and searches for instant panaceas lose sight of these essentials.

Each school is unique. Although there are obviously major similarities among schools, the mix of administrators, teachers, and students, and the expectations of and connections to local communities, are particular to each school setting. This setting, with the people who live there every day – the students, teachers, and administrators – is the best unit for educational change. The culture of an individual school may not be supportive of learning, but it is the place to begin.

Too often, programs to improve teaching are designed apart from, and then imposed upon, the school. Seeing it as an imposition, teachers in the school rarely adopt the program; they fail to "own" it, and the reform does not become part of their repertoire. In contrast, as a Rand Corporation study of federally funded school reforms notes, the most successful school improvement projects of the last two decades were "an integral part of an ongoing problem-solving and improvement process within the school." They were part of what the individual school was already doing to improve itself.[13]

The improvement of teaching methods, more effective classroom management techniques, the use of new technologies, and the improvement of school climate are best done in the individual school. But these changes will not occur automatically. Schools are not equally good: Teaching staffs are not equally competent, and the desire for renewal is not equally distributed. Individual schools do not exist in isolation, nor should they pull up their drawbridges and attempt to solve their problems on their own. The view that only those on site know what to do is too narrow; outside perspectives provide insights often missed by those on location. The changes in schools can be sustained only if they are supported from outside the schools by central administrators, parents, and legislators.

Improving the practice of teaching thus requires collaborative planning, which begins with accepting the legitimacy of the work that teachers are already doing. Teachers accommodate to their perceptions of the best interests of their students and of themselves. They are not always right, but they are also not always wrong, as critics of teachers sometimes imply. Much of what teachers do needs to be supported and sustained, yet at the same time teachers need incentives to change their practice. In both cases, concern about teaching must begin with what teachers actually do and the ways they think and understand their practice.

Reflecting upon a curriculum/pedagogical reform program, one teacher commented, "I wished . . . they had asked teachers, 'What have you already done that's working?' It seems strange that in two years they haven't asked me anything."[14] Another teacher made a similar point about a different program, complaining that the project divided the faculty. "This was the result of forcing a program on a school, using an outside coordinator unfamiliar with the school and faculty, and not having the full support of teachers." Paradoxically, the ideas of the project were good and could have worked had the teachers not been excluded from the planning.[15]

Involving teachers in the planning process acknowledges and incorporates the valuable practices they already engage in and seeks to further their commitment to improving practice. It does not seem to matter whether teachers, principals, or central administrators initiate the ideas for change. The important thing is that the idea is considered and implemented with the full participation of all groups. Summarizing the Rand Corporation study, Milbrey McLaughlin and David Marsh conclude that the commitment of teachers to the goals of a project "had the most consistently positive relationship to all of the project outcomes, e.g., percentage of project goals achieved, change in teachers, change in student performance, and continuation of project methods and materials."[16] Involving teachers in planning goals and strategies for the institution as a whole and for their practice as teachers enables them to play vital roles in the long-term development and improvement of their school. Yet collaborative planning should also extend beyond the professionals in the school. All who have a stake in the changes should be included: parents, community groups, students, local businesses and cultural organizations, neighboring colleges.

Such tasks are not easily accomplished. Leaving aside the complexities of involving a multitude of agencies in the schools, the organization of most schools does not easily lend itself to an open-ended process in which teachers have a voice in determining the nature of practice. Teachers, with some justification, are wary of administrators, experts, and community activists who propose programs whereby teachers are "improved." Little financial support exists for efforts to renew teaching; only when a crisis is discovered, as in the shortage of mathematics and science teachers, do funds become available, though more often, in practice, existing teachers are asked to resolve that crisis without additional resources. Faced with increasing demands for cost-effective spending, school boards find it difficult to justify expenditures on long-term programs to improve teaching when the effects are difficult to prove and the results may not be immediate, measurable, or politically satisfying. The present concern for teacher accountability accentuates this difficulty, increasing pressure to measure teacher performance by student test scores. Simplistic and far from inerrant, accountability reinforces the worst tendencies in teaching: teaching for tests, overrelying on limited measures of achievement; overvaluing credentials; and stultifying inquiry, experimentation, and reflection. As a means of increasing teachers' willing participation in the improvement of their teaching, accountability is not a very promising incentive.

Motivating the majority of teachers to participate in collaborative planning is a perennial problem. After years of exclusion, teachers distrust administrators' motives. Collegial governance is highly time-consuming and requires a commitment beyond school hours that may come only when teachers believe that the extra effort required pays off. On the few occasions that presently exist for collaborative planning, many teachers fail to take a part. "The same old few" is the familiar refrain. And those who do not participate are often the teachers most in need of professional renewal. As many issues related to collegial governance become part of collective bargaining agreements, collegiality becomes a double-edged sword: The more responsibility for governance of schools that teachers win, the more their reluctant or recalcitrant colleagues become their responsibility.

Although none of these obstacles to collaborative planning is insurmountable, neither is any one of them easily overcome. If new collaborative models are to be implemented successfully, strong leadership is needed. This leadership can come from a number of sources. Dedicated school principals can win the trust and support of teachers, share power and responsibility with them, and keep bureaucracy to a minimum. Career ladders and master teacher programs may help by giving outstanding teachers recognition and authority to engage their colleagues in efforts to improve teaching. Colleges and universities can offer advice and assistance to school-based programs without taking over control of them. Central administrators and school boards can justify expenditures to allow teachers to collaborate on their teaching by explaining their roles in improving the quality of teaching.

One way to start is for all groups involved in education to acknowledge that good teaching is an art as well as a technique. The outcomes of teaching are elusive; no one method is right; experiments do not always succeed. Too often, in the desire to find the path to effective schools and effective teaching, the technocratic mentality of schooling triumphs. The problem is defined as the need to improve scores on standardized aptitude and achievement tests; the resolution is for teachers to present clear academic goals, concentrate their energies on instructional tasks, organize and extensively cover the subject matter, closely monitor student progress and adapt their curriculum materials in that light, require frequent and quick feedback from students on what they have learned, and limit classroom disturbances to a minimum. These are standard techniques of teaching that each teacher will occasionally resort to as guides in teaching. Taken by themselves, they represent a simple analysis of the problem with simple prescriptions of how to resolve it.[17]

Seen as part of the repertoire of instructional behaviors, such prescriptions serve a useful purpose. They give clear messages and undoubtedly help teachers assume greater control of their classrooms. But if used too narrowly, they limit teaching to the easily measurable and become inflexible prescriptions – a series of steps to be taken, like adding ingredients according to a cookbook. Such an approach to teaching suggests that teachers should follow a standardized routine that will somehow guarantee the product.

But that is not all that teaching is about, at least not the best teaching. Teachers treat individual students differently. They ought to, not in the sense of discriminating against them, but by responding to and expanding upon their different needs, abilities, and personalities. Teachers manifest these same differences; they too have different attributes that affect their teaching. The tendency to apply narrow educational research findings focused on achieving limited goals as a panacea to be adopted by every teacher with every child tries to transform teaching into a technocratic process, dismissing the necessary adaptation of practice to the distinctiveness of individual classrooms. In their nearly exclusive emphasis on achieving better test scores, these teaching recommendations inflexibly narrow the definition of learning. And they create an illusion about the certainty of outcomes in a craft that is rooted in uncertainty, even in the most highly structured environments.

Teaching is more than a repertoire of specific skills. It is more than a teacher teaching a student. Rather, it is an interactive process – a conversation – whereby teachers teach something to someone and simultaneously are taught something by someone else. "All teaching," John Passmore writes, "is pupil-centered in the sense that its object is not merely to expound a subject but to help somebody learn something . . . at the same time as the teacher is trying to teach pupils *something* and it is by no means unimportant what that something is." The teacher has to teach both students and subjects, and to do that, he or she must "reconcile respect for the child and respect for what is being taught."[18]

In Chapter 4 we described the curriculum as a conversation, the content of which is a mixture of facts and values to which teachers and students interact. Unfortunately, we often think of the curriculum simply as something teachers teach and students learn, and thus neglect its conversational and interactive quality. The explicit dimensions of a curriculum (its subject matter) and the implicit content (its values, norms, expectations) interact as teachers and students engage with one another. The outcomes are not predictable. The knowledge may not be received by the students; the teacher may be teaching and the students not learning; what is received may be used in ways for which it was not intended. Teachers and administrators may decide what students will be expected to learn, but they have to recognize that what students actually learn will be negotiated in practice. This negotiated interactive process makes it almost impossible, and not very useful, to separate subject matter from the act of teaching itself. The oft-heard distinction between teaching the subject and teaching the child makes almost no sense at all – something John Dewey recognized almost a century ago.

Teaching something to someone presumes diversity, adaptability, and respect for what Israel Scheffler calls "the student's intellectual integrity and capacity for independent judgment."[19] The answers to the questions of how something is taught, why it is taught, when it is taught, what is taught, and by whom it is taught will vary. They should vary, for the art of teaching requires sensitivity to the variegated nature of the learning process. The goal is not to dismiss and diminish that variety, but to establish the conditions for its enlargement. Only then can the promise of teaching be fulfilled.

7

THINKING ABOUT REFORM

HISTORY rarely tells us anything specific about the present. It offers no programs. Its lessons are seldom clear, always subject to interpretations. In this sense, historian Carl Becker's aphorism, "Each man his own historian," is persuasive. We have argued in this book that the past can give us insight into present dilemmas about education. History can help us understand how and why we face the issues we do, and can suggest ways to frame questions about the present that make more sense than those that ignore the historical record. Where we have been and where we are likely to go form a continuous dialogue, involving our intellects and our passions.

On some issues, the history of American education is especially revealing. The first is that there was never a golden age of the past. The tendency in recent years has been to point to some earlier period in American history, usually vaguely defined, during which the schools functioned well, when teachers taught, students learned, academic knowledge was prized, and families were supportive of what teachers did. When public criticism, in short, hardly existed.

The historical record reveals quite the contrary. The range of criticism, the persistent efforts to reform education from the early nineteenth century on, suggest that Americans have never been satisfied with their schools. How could they have been? In the nineteenth century, Americans were often caught up in religious and ethnic controversies, in the divisions over slavery, in the place of women as citizens, in the fragmenting effects of a people constantly on the move, a people caught between competing beliefs in individualism and community. The schools reflected and refracted those controversies. They had to if they were to be considered important.

What happened in the twentieth century was not a new appearance of controversy and criticism, but the intensification of criticisms about the responsibility of schools to promote social mobility. This role was not entirely new, nor did it eliminate continued criticisms over the religious and ethnic values of the schools. But it did modify the stakes. To the extent that students leaving school did not fulfill their own or others' economic expectations, schools were seen to be failing. To the extent that the nation was seen to be losing its economic and military dominance to other nations, schools were seen to be failing.

These changes had the effect of shifting the focus of many of the criticisms of public schools away from the religious and ethnic issues that once dominated. The changes had the additional effect of shifting the locus of controversy from local communities to state, regional, and federal levels. Schools were still embedded in local politics, but they had also become the concern of the nation at large.

Americans have been highly critical of their schools for a long, long time. Whatever lessons the educational past teaches us, a golden age when the schools were all right is not one of them. The public schools have been especially controversial, for they have been the one place where Americans have articulated a common good. In no other institution have so many hopes for the future been placed. Nowhere else have Americans engaged their private interests, what all individuals want for themselves, or their children, or their neighbors' children, against larger community interests. The juxtaposition of private and public interests has been at the heart of some of the most contentious battles over education.

Sometimes combining public and private desires seemed too difficult; private interests were unable to be accommodated in a common setting. Under these conditions, many Americans turned to private schools of a particular religion, nationality, or social class. Indeed, private education has played an important role in American life, providing opportunities alongside the common system. Private schools have been, and continue to be, essential to the notion of choice within the educational process. But they do not extend the commitment to common goals. The overwhelming number of Americans have remained within the public schools, bringing their expectations and frustrations into them. They have been forced to confront the question, "How can we forge commonality in a pluralist society?"

The educational past reveals that the conflicts and criticisms of public schools are inherent in the idea of seeking a common education in a pluralist society. The controversial nature of public education will not disappear. At least it will not disappear unless we cease to believe that schools are important. That is an option, of course, but one not likely to occur. We must confront, then, the central paradox of public education: As long as public schools remain important, what happens in them will be controversial. The problem is to debate the multiple purposes of public education and reach compromises that allow the commitments to public schooling to remain strong and the public schools to flourish. Understanding our educational past will make its important lessons active and illuminating forces in our current debates.

THE TWIN CHALLENGES

It is time to recognize in more than just rhetorical terms that schools ought to be committed to enhancing equality and promoting excellence. The two challenges are part of their mission; they represent the collective and accumulated aspirations that Americans have for schooling. Educational debates should not be about whether the goals are worthwhile, but about how to accomplish them. Equality and excellence ought to be the assumed ends of education; educational policy ought to be the means.

To make these debates about the means effective, we need to remember that any definitions of equality and excellence will be controversial. They should be, for the issues are fundamental to American society. In a diverse society like ours, there is no way to establish a single definition of equality and excellence, at least not one of any substance. In a society that changes as consistently as ours, our definitions need to anticipate change and conflict, frustrations and imperfections. The definitions should be multifaceted and flexible. Seeking ends that are easily measurable or absolute will narrow our understanding of education and reduce our ability and willingness to change.

Intelligence is a many-faceted phenomenon. Schools that seek to prize intelligence can do so only if they prize its many forms. Students' expectations, interests, learning styles, and capacities vary greatly. Schools ought to recognize these differences and indeed glory in the variety rather than treating them as problems. The twin challenges of equality and excellence cannot be met by simple and easily measurable methods like counting the number of racial minorities or giving standardized written examinations, though either of these may be valuable in concrete situations in which the aims are quite specifically defined. But the twin challenges of schooling are not so easily met and should not be so narrowly conceived.

A view of equality and excellence that stresses their fluidity and variations undoubtedly leaves us uncertain. How do we know when we have achieved both, or even one or the other? How do we even know when we are moving in the right direction? The answer to the first question is that Americans are not likely to believe, certainly not in the near future, that they have achieved either equality or excellence. They will have to live with that unsettling realization, acknowledging that ambiguity in the achievement of ends is not the same as being unable to recognize the direction being taken.

We may be uncertain about the most appropriate definitions of equality and excellence in education, but we can determine when we are moving away from rather than toward those goals. In Chapter 3, for example, we discussed the way tracking programs often serve to undermine our commitments to equality and excellence by almost any definition most Americans would accept. As presently constituted, most tracking programs do not enhance the learning experience of the students involved, especially for those students who are tracked into the lowest groups. They serve mainly to segregate students without making a commitment to increase their skills or their desire to learn. Unless clear learning gains can be achieved by such practices, we see little reason to have them. The onus of proof should be on those who wish to segregate.

The concern for excellence should not become a commitment simply to the winners in school. If seeking excellence means the provision of special programs, the best teachers, and increased funding for the students with the highest test scores, excellence will be achieved at the expense of equality and will eventually become a source of conflict itself. Instead, we need to see excellence, as we suggested in Chapter 4, in terms of developing the skills and capacities of all students and achieving levels of learning all too rarely attained by any students. Basic skills – the ability to read, write, compute, and engage in oral communication – and basic knowledge of literature, history, science, and the host of other subjects we want students to understand are all necessary. That belief ought to be presumed in the activities of schools.

But beyond those skills and types of knowledge, and indeed integral to them, are capacities like critical thinking and imaginative expression, which are essential if we are to have excellence in schools.

The tendency to separate the basic skills from imaginative and critical thinking drastically undermines the opportunity to achieve the basics and narrows our commitment to excellence. One failure of our schools is the large number of students who leave them each year without basic skills. But that is part of a larger failure – the inability of the schools to impart a commitment to learning. Without that commitment, few students will be persuaded to learn anything beyond the basics, and all too many will see little reason to learn even those.

Finally, it is important to recognize that there will always be tension between equality and excellence. In any institution, choices are made over what to fund, to whom to give attention, what should be rewarded, and in what ways. Just as it will be impossible always to agree on what is meant by equality and excellence, so too will there be times when preference will be given to one side of the equation rather than the other. What is important at these times, however, is that we be honest about the nature of those choices, that they be openly arrived at, and that the costs and the gains be acknowledged, as well as the uncertainties. The choices need to be seen as part of a continuing adjustment process, a process that is inevitable in any social institution. If we can recognize that, we will not be fooled into thinking that we have eliminated the tension between equality and excellence. In a democratic society, that tension is ineradicable.

THE REFORM AGENDA

In articulating the view that the schools ought to be committed to equality and excellence, this book has offered a number of suggestions. These do not constitute a definitive handbook of what to do; it would be a mistake to view them as implying that there is a simple way to transpose analysis into programs. Much more important than the specific reforms we champion at any particular moment are the ways we think about and talk about the schools and the ways we approach the improvement of education.

This book has focused on certain vital issues for reform. Organizational practices such as tracking, which decrease the likelihood that students will be pushed to the limits of their capabilities, undermine the commitment to learning necessary for a vital educational system. Computers can aid learning, but to do so they must be available to all, a challenge that will certainly require more extensive funding by the states and, in all probability, greater federal investments. Basic skills should be seen as part of our larger notion of literacy. We should recognize that teaching involves learning.

But beyond these and other suggestions found in the preceding chapters, other aspects of the reform agenda need elaboration: developing school identities, improving the quality of teaching, establishing environments conducive to learning, and invigorating educational leadership. Individual schools need a reason for being. They ought to have points of view, guiding principles that give them an identity and shape what they do. Private schools often, though not always, have such identities. Occasionally, a public school will have one. It is a place that stands for something. But much more often, the school lacks principles to guide it. The individuals in these schools point to bureaucratic reasons or to externally imposed requirements to justify what they do or do not do. Rarely do the people within a particular school ask, "What does our school stand for?"

The question needs to be posed. Answering it requires that teachers reflect on why they are teaching and what their purposes are. It requires administrators to assess the goals of their administration and decide what they would like their schools to do. Students will need to ask why they are learning (or not learning) and seek to understand the many ways and purposes of learning. And parents and other citizens will need to decide why they support (or do not support) the schools.

Too many schools fall prey to whatever is fashionable, and too readily take responsibility for whatever is the current social problem. But schools that make a commitment to some guiding principles can use them to choose among the myriad innovations, criticisms, and programs that are always ready to overwhelm educators. A school that has an identity and a sense of mission can determine whether the new program or the current fad is likely to further the purposes of the school. Perhaps most importantly, schools that have identities are more likely to capture the loyalty and commitment of those who teach and learn in them. That is crucial: A school that fosters loyalty and commitment from its students and teachers has a chance to be a school in which learning is valued.

Improvement should begin with the conditions under which most teachers teach. Those who do not teach can barely understand the lack of privacy, the emotional drains, the constant need to shift emotions, to adjust expectations and plans, and to respond to the human dimensions of about 30 children a day in the elementary school and over 120 daily in the high school. It is also difficult to understand the effects on teachers of public discussions of education that almost invariably condemn the teachers. The real wonder is not that the quality of teaching is low, but that so many good teachers remain and that creative teaching continues to occur.

Improving the quality of teaching will involve enhancing and rewarding those already doing outstanding jobs, challenging and helping those who are not, and attracting outstanding individuals into teaching. In effect, two questions need to be answered: How can we change conditions so that teachers can perform to the best of their abilities? How can we attract and retain talented teachers? The questions are not the same, but they are interrelated.

The simplest answer to both questions is to raise the salaries of teachers. Discussions on improving the quality of teaching are meaningless if we are unwilling to pay teachers substantially more. For better or worse, respect of a profession in America is accorded on the basis of income. Paying teachers more is a statement of our respect for what they do. Without granting higher salaries, it will remain exceedingly difficult to attract and retain talented individuals. That has become especially true now that large numbers of talented women once attracted to teaching because there were few opportunities elsewhere are entering more lucrative and prestigious professions. It is unimportant whether we build more elaborate career ladders into the teaching profession or establish merit pay to reward the most outstanding teachers. It is much more important that we increase salaries substantially for all teachers.

Increased salaries are necessary, but insufficient. Significant improvements in the preparation of teachers are also needed. To put it bluntly, teacher preparation is poor. The quality of undergraduate schools of education often leaves much to be desired. But the problem goes beyond that, because most teachers have limited contact with education courses. Elementary school teachers, for example, take about 40% of their courses in education, whereas high school teachers take only 20%. The role of undergraduate schools of education will likely be reduced even further in favor of more arts and sciences courses and increased amounts of time spent in internships in schools.

Improving the quality of teacher preparation then means raising serious questions about the quality of education in the arts and sciences. Far too many students complete English courses with little knowledge of literature; those taking history courses have been exposed only to bland textbooks; and those taking mathematics and science courses think that completing laboratory workbooks is the equivalent of laboratory experimentation. Insufficient attention has been given to just how deadening the quality of teaching and coursework is in many undergraduate institutions. To become creative teachers themselves, college students first need to be inspired by their own professors.

Paying greater attention to the training of teachers will help to improve the quality of teaching in schools. But teacher training is not the major issue. The problem lies much more substantially with what goes on in schools. Many teachers overcome poor preparation. Many of the best prepared and most promising entrants soon become mediocre teachers. The more productive approach, as we have asserted throughout this book, is to think of teaching itself as a process of learning.

Few individuals can retain a commitment to the transmission of knowledge unless they themselves are involved in learning. For teachers, that means being able to teach under conditions that give them the time, the incentive, and the freedom to explore subject matter. It means smaller classes, not because students in small classes necessarily learn more, but because smaller classes allow teachers flexibility in thinking about the material, exploring it, and adapting it to the differing needs and learning styles of students. Such freedom will always be subject to constraints; the economic costs of more time, smaller classes, and more privacy are substantial. But if we are not willing to pay some of these costs, we should not expect significant improvements in the quality of teaching. Certainly there will be constraints imposed by legislative demands, though these rarely have much effect on what actually goes on in classrooms other than to curb the sense of autonomy and responsibility that teachers ought to feel for their own teaching. Parents and other interest groups that care about what happens in the schools will claim considerable stake in what is taught.

Teachers are always constrained in their need to balance the demands that come from outside the classroom with their own sense of what is appropriate for themselves and their students. This constraint is an essential condition of teaching in a democratic society, in which large numbers of persons have a stake in the educational system. But in the rush to make teaching better and to demand that teachers be more accountable, teachers often find themselves tightly trussed by constraints, even well-intentioned ones. The emphasis should be instead on providing incentives for teachers to shape existing curricula so that the subject matter they care about can be pursued more fully in a variety of ways. Too often, instead of incentives, teachers are handed a rigid curriculum, complete with standardized tests that are treated as evaluations of them as much as evaluations of how much the students have learned. There is little in the past experiences of schools to suggest that the quality of teaching will be improved by these means. Nor will more creative and committed teachers be attracted into teaching.

Along with freedom comes the responsibility of teachers to live up to the autonomy accorded professionals. With the right to experiment and be creative, to treat the classroom as a place where both teachers and students learn, comes the responsibility to learn and to teach. Teachers who do not know their subject matter, who fail to engage their students, or who otherwise fail to respond to the freedom to be teachers should not be tolerated. Teachers' organizations must share that responsibility much more than they do now. There will be disagreements about how to determine whether a teacher is meeting his or her responsibilities. Different points of view surround any evaluative system. We should not be afraid of differences, but we need to be clear on what we are disagreeing about and to establish mechanisms for reaching agreement. We should make sure that the evaluative system – whatever it is – seeks to promote improved teaching and learning for both teachers and students. Unless teachers' organizations take part in shaping, perhaps even dominating, the evaluative mechanisms of teaching, they will continue in their current predicament, defensively responding to most calls for change by seeking to undermine or postpone them. The freedom to engage in active learning with their students can be gained only if teachers simultaneously take on the responsibility to challenge and aid those peers who are not teaching, or not teaching well. Only in this way can teaching become the dignified, creative, and responsible activity it ought to be.

This process can be furthered by paying greater attention to the environments of learning. In previous chapters, we stressed the interactive, conversational qualities of teaching and learning. These are enhanced by intimate learning environments, which are best – though not always exclusively – created in small settings. The tendency during the 1950s and 1960s to construct large schools and the more current trend toward closing small schools because they are uneconomical have made it extremely difficult to create conducive settings for learning. Large school buildings, especially at the high school level, may provide gymnasiums, auditoriums, industrial shops, home economics rooms, computer workshops, and the host of other facilities that presumably define a good school. But much more important than expensive equipment and facilities is the sense of involvement and community that comes with smaller, manageable groupings and that can aid the process of mutual learning among teachers and students. It is usually better to provide fewer courses and less specialized programs than to lose the intimacy and flexibility frequently found in small schools. If special facilities are necessary, they can be provided in more specialized buildings. They do not need to be a part of the setting in which students spend most of their learning day.

In addition to restructuring the environments for learning, we need to revise our understanding of educational leadership. Because the most important and effective changes take place at the school level, the methods of selecting and educating principals should be seriously reconsidered. Principals set the tone and terms of learning in their schools. It is hard to imagine that learning and teaching can be held in high esteem if the people chosen to lead the schools do not have high levels of learning and excellent records of teaching achievement. Principals should have mastery of some of the subjects taught in their schools. They should be superior teachers, which is far more important than having extra education courses to their credit. The practice of choosing principals based primarily – and sometimes, it seems, exclusively – on the fact that they are good disciplinarians, run the football team well, or organize paperwork effectively should end. Principals should articulate a vision of what ought to be learned and should engage teachers, students, parents, and the community in discussions of what is educative. They themselves should be actively involved in learning and should be committed to developing learning opportunities for their teachers. Above all, principals should be responsible for creating the conditions that allow teachers to initiate and sustain improvements in schools.

These tasks will not be easy. Principals work with few resources and many restraints, and in the face of opposition and apathy. Their days are often consumed with details and punctuated by emergencies demanding their immediate response. In this atmosphere, they will find it tempting to search for a technological fix or to seize as a panacea the partial answers and explanations provided by educational research. But their responsibility is to see through the details to the larger purposes of schooling.

The leadership of principals is essential to the improvement of schooling, but it is not, in itself, sufficient. If American education is to be substantially strengthened, there must be renewed public commitment to public education. In recent years, the common interest in public schooling has been stretched thin. Schools run the gauntlet of single-interest politics, with each group out for itself. Voucher systems, tuition tax credits, and limits on government taxation and spending threaten to divide public support further. Without advocates, public schooling is in danger of unraveling into schools with single constituencies: ghetto schools for the urban poor, private schools for the children of the wealthy, Spanish-speaking schools for Hispanic students, religious academies, and racially segregated institutions.

There are, however, encouraging hints that coalitions in support of the public schools are reemerging. In cities like Boston and Denver, well-publicized campaigns have been mounted to resist cutbacks and to enhance public support for the schools. Business and labor groups have invested time and money to improve educational programs. Many governors and legislatures are giving renewed attention to public education and are recommending increased funding for schools. But strong public schools also require federal commitments. Equality and excellence are national concerns. The health of our schools is simply too important to be neglected by the federal government.

These and other developments hold promise for the resuscitation of public schooling. The determination to find sustenance at the local level is especially heartening. Active school–community relations can enhance the teaching capacity of a school's staff, the school's climate for learning, and the attitudes and learning opportunities of its students. But if local groups are to develop any significant clout, they must work together to ensure that education has a plurality of strong advocates at the state and federal levels.

This advocacy for public education should be directed toward enhancing the school's educative power. By educative power, we do not mean the school's power to command public budgets, or pupil attendance, or even allegiance to its purposes, although these powers are important. What we do mean by educative power is the school's ability to challenge, motivate, instruct, and develop students' and teachers' abilities and attitudes, its power to excite and engage them in learning and growing.

It is hard for Americans to believe in the value of learning for its own sake; we seem to need an extraordinary number of justifications. It is legitimate to expect the schools to contribute to economic growth, to occupational success, to the articulation of common and personal values, and to an active and knowledgeable citizenship. We should encourage and help schools to play these roles. But we should value learning as its own end. The desire to know still more and the skills to gain that knowledge are what schools should be about. Beyond the specifics of any particular school or course of study, the desire and ability to continue learning are the real benefits of an education of value.

NOTES

Chapter 1

1. Lawrence A. Cremin, *American Education: The National Experience, 1783–1876* (New York: Harper & Row, 1980); Carl Kaestle, *Pillars of the Schools: Common Schools and American Society, 1780–1860* (New York: Hill and Wang, 1983).

2. David B. Tyack, *The One-Best System: A History of American Urban Education* (Cambridge, Mass.: Harvard University Press, 1974), ch. 1. See also Patricia Albjerg Graham, *Community and Class in American Education, 1865–1915* (New York: Wiley, 1974), ch. 2.

· 3. Diane Ravitch, *The Great School Wars: New York City, 1805–1973* (New York: Basic Books, 1974), chs. 1–7; Marvin Lazerson, "Understanding American Catholic Educational History," *History of Education Quarterly* 17 (Fall 1977), 297–317; Stanley Schultz, *The Culture Factory: Boston Public Schools, 1798–1860* (New York: Oxford University Press, 1973); David A. Gerber, *Black Ohio and the Color Line, 1860–1915* (Urbana: Illinois University Press, 1976).

4. Leon Litwack, *Been in the Storm So Long: The Aftermath of Slavery* (New York: Knopf, 1979), ch. 9.

5. Ibid.

6. Larry Cuban, "Teacher as Leader and Captive: Continuity and Change in American Classrooms, 1890–1980," ch. 1 (ERIC System: National Institute of Education, Grant No. NIE G-81-0024, 1982). See also Barbara Finkelstein, "Reading, Writing, and the Acquisition of Identity in the United States: 1790–1860," in Finkelstein (ed.), *Regulated Children/Liberated Children: Education in Psychohistorical Perspective* (New York: Psychohistory Press, 1979).

7. Leonard P. Ayres, *Laggards in Our Schools: A Study of Retardation and Elimination in City School Systems* (New York: Charities Publication Committee, 1908).

8. Oscar Handlin, *Race and Nationality in American Life* (Boston: Beacon Press, 1957).

9. Stephen Jay Gould, *The Mismeasure of Man* (New York: Norton, 1981), pp. 151–2.

10. Ibid., p. 157.

11. Quoted in Paul Chapman, "Schools as Sorters: Lewis M. Terman and the Intelligence Testing Movement, 1890–1930," doctoral dissertation, Stanford University, 1979.

12. Tyack, *The One-Best System*, pp. 198–229.

13. National Society for the Study of Education, *The Grouping of Pupils Yearbook*, pt. 1 (Bloomington, Ill.: NSSE, 1936).

14. Marvin Lazerson, "The Origins of Special Education," in Jay Chambers and William Hartman (eds.), *Special Education Policies: Their History, Implementation, and Finance* (Philadelphia: Temple University Press, 1982).

15. Tyack, *The One-Best System*, pt 1.

16. Ibid.

17. See Sara Lawrence Lightfoot, *Worlds Apart: Relationships Between Families and Schools* (New York: Basic Books, 1978); Joseph and Helen Featherstone, "Partners and Antagonists," *Working Papers for a Democratic Society* (May–June 1978), 8–10.

18. David Hogan, "Education and the Making of the Chicago Working Class, 1880–1930," *History of Education Quarterly* 18 (1978), 227–270.

19. W. Norton Grubb and Marvin Lazerson, *Broken Promises: How Americans Fail Their Children* (New York: Basic Books, 1982), chs. 4, 5.

20. "Report of the Committee of Ten on Secondary School Studies," in Daniel Calhoun (ed.), *The Educating of Americans: A Documentary History* (Boston: Houghton Mifflin, 1969), pp. 477–83.

21. "Cardinal Principles of Secondary Education: A Report of the Commission on the Reorganization of Secondary Education" and reports of subcommittees in ibid., pp. 485–505.

22. Robert and Helen Lynd, *Middletown* (New York: Harcourt, Brace and World, 1929).

23. James B. Conant, *The American High School Today* (New York: McGraw-Hill, 1957).

24. Carl Kaestle and Mari Vinovskis, *Education and Social Change in Nineteenth-Century Massachusetts* (Cambridge: Cambridge University Press, 1980), ch. 4; Harvey Kantor and David Tyack (eds.), *Work, Youth and Schooling: Historical Perspectives on Vocationalism* (Stanford, Calif.: Stanford University Press, 1982).

25. Horatio Alger, *Ragged Dick* (New York: Collier, 1962 ed.), pp. 135, 165.

26. This and the following paragraphs are based on W. Norton Grubb and Marvin Lazerson, "Education and the Labor Market: Recycling the Youth Problem," in Kantor and Tyack, *Work, Youth and Schooling*.

27. Lynd, *Middletown*, p. 11; David Tyack, Robert Lowe, and Elizabeth

Hansot, *Public Schools in Hard Times: The Great Depression and Recent Years* (Cambridge, Mass.: Harvard University Press, 1984), pp. 172–3.

28. Tyack, *The One-Best System,* pp. 123–4; Tyack et al., *Public Schools,* pp. 174–85.

29. Cremin, *National Experience,* p. 104.

30. Diane Ravitch, *The Troubled Crusade: American Education, 1945–1980* (New York: Basic Books, 1983).

Chapter 2

1. Jerome Bruner, *The Process of Education* (Cambridge, Mass.: Harvard University Press, 1960), p. vii.

2. On the curriculum reform movement in the sciences, see Philip Jackson, "The Reform of Science Education: A Cautionary Tale," *Daedalus* 112 (Spring 1983), 143–66; and Paul E. Marsh, "The Physical Science Study Committee: A Case History of Nationwide Curriculum Development, 1956–1961," Ed. D. dissertation, Harvard Graduate School of Education, 1964. On the English curriculum, see Herbert Muller, *The Uses of English* (New York: Holt, Rinehart and Winston, 1967); and John Dixon, *Growth Through English* (New York: Oxford University Press, 1967).

3. William Wooten, *SMSG, the Making of a Curriculum* (New Haven, Conn.: Yale University Press, 1965), p. 10. Unless otherwise noted, this account of the SMSG is drawn from Wooten.

4. College Entrance Examination Board, Commission on Mathematics, *Program for College Preparatory Mathematics* (New York: CEEB, 1959).

5. Edward Begle, "SMSG: Where We Are Today," in Elliot Eisner (ed.), *Confronting Curriculum Reform* (Boston: Little, Brown, 1971), p. 76.

6. Donald J. Dessart, "Curriculum," in Elizabeth Fennera (ed.), *Mathematics Education Research: Implications for the '80s* (Alexandria, Va.: Association for Supervision and Curriculum Development, 1981), pp. 10–11.

7. Wooten. *SMSG,* p. 136.

8. Seymour Sarason, *The Culture of the School and the Problem of Change* (Boston: Allyn and Bacon, 1982), pp. 41–2.

9. Tom Lehrer, "That Was the Year That Was," recorded July 1965 at the Hungry I, San Francisco, words and music by Tom Lehrer, all songs: ASCAP. Reprise Records RS 6179.

10. This account of *Man: A Course of Study* is drawn from Peter Dow, "Innovation's Perils: An Account of the Origins, Development, Implementation, and Public Reaction to *Man: A Course of Study,*" doctoral dissertation, Harvard Graduate School of Education, 1979.

11. *Man: A Course of Study* (Cambridge, Mass.: Education Development Center, © 1968, 1969, 1970). Disseminated and produced by Curriculum Development Associates, Washington, D.C.

12. *Man: A Course of Study, A Guide to the Course* (Cambridge, Mass.: Education Development Center, 1970), pp. 5–7.

13. Dow, "Innovation's Perils," pp. 372–5.

14. Ibid., p. 299.

15. *"Man: A Course of Study,* Abstract of Evaluation Studies," distributed by Curriculum Development Associates, pp. 1–4.

16. This and the other controversies are described in Dow, "Innovation's Perils," p. 396.

17. Ibid., p. 252; Dorothy Nelkin, *Science Textbook Controversies and the Politics of Equal Time* (Cambridge, Mass.: MIT Press, 1977), p. 112.

18. Bruner, *The Process of Education,* p. 33.

19. National Science Foundation, *The Status of Pre-College Science, Mathematics, and Social Studies Education in the United States, 1955–1975,* Vols. I–III (Washington, D.C.: U.S. Government Printing Office, 1980); Stanley Helgeson, Robert Stake, Iris Weiss, et al., *The Status of Pre-College Science, Mathematics and Social Studies Educational Practices in U.S. Schools: An Overview and Summaries of Three Studies* (Washington, D.C.: U.S. Government Printing Office, 1978); Iris Weiss, *Report of the 1977 National Survey of Science, Mathematics and Social Studies Education* (Washington, D.C.: U.S. Government Printing Office, 1978); Robert E. Stake, Jack Easley, et al., *Case Studies in Secondary Education,* Vols. I and II (Washington, D.C.: U.S. Government Printing Office, 1978); National Science Foundation (NSF), *What Are the Needs in Pre-College Science, Mathematics, and Social Science Education? Views from the Field* (Washington, D.C.: U.S. Government Printing Office, 1979). The quotations are from *What Are the Needs?* pp. 22, 23; Stake, Easley, et al., Vol. II, pp. 13, 23.

20. NSF, *What Are the Needs?* p. 6.

21. See, for example, Neil Postman and Charles Weingartner, *Teaching as a Subversive Activity* (New York: Dell, 1969); Jerry Farber, *The Student as Nigger* (New York: Pocket Books. 1970).

22. Sarason, *Culture of the School,* p. 40.

23. These issues are discussed in NSF, *The Status of Pre-College Science,* Vol. III, pp. 22–48; National Council of Teachers of Mathematics, *A History of Mathematics Education in the United States and Canada, 32nd Yearbook* (Washington, D.C.: NCTM, 1970) pp. 455–60; Lawrence Stenhouse, "Social Science Education in the United States, 1955–1975, A British Perspective," *Proceedings of the National Academy of Education* 7 (1980), pp. 102–6.

24. Rita Peterson, "Science Education in the United States During the Third Quarter of the Twentieth Century," *Proceedings of the National Academy of Education* 7 (1980), 29, 69.

Chapter 3

1. Quoted in David B. Tyack, *Turning Points in American Educational History* (Boston: Blaisdel, 1967), pp. 140–1.
2. Stanley Schultz, *The Culture Factory: Boston Public Schools, 1789–1860* (New York: Oxford University Press, 1973).
3. This theme has been developed by numerous historians, but most especially by Lawrence A. Cremin, *American Education: The National Experience, 1783–1876* (New York: Harper & Row, 1980).
4. Carl Kaestle and Maris Vinovskis, *Education and Social Change in Nineteenth-Century Massachusetts* (Cambridge: Cambridge University Press, 1980), ch. 4.
5. David K. Cohen and Barbara Neufeld, "The Failure of High Schools and the Progress of Education," *Daedalus* 110 (Summer 1981), 69–89.
6. John Dewey, *Democracy and Education* (New York: Macmillan, 1916), ch. 4.
7. Michael Walzer, *Radical Principles: Reflections of an Unreconstructed Democrat* (New York: Basic Books, 1980), p. 239. See also Howard Gardner, *Frames of Mind: A Theory of Multiple Intelligences* (New York: Basic Books, 1983).
8. See Karl L. Alexander, Martha Cook, and Edward L. McDill, "Curriculum Tracking and Educational Stratification: Some Further Evidence," *American Sociological Review* 43 (February 1978), 47–55; Warren Findley and Miriam M. Bryan, *Ability Grouping 1970: Status, Implications, and Alternatives* (Athens, Ga.: Center for Educational Improvement, 1971); John Goodlad, *A Place Called School* (New York: McGraw-Hill, 1983); Barbara Heyns, "Social Selection and Stratification within Schools," *American Journal of Sociology* 76 (May 1974), 1434–51; Richard A. Rehlberg and Evelyn R. Rosenthal, *Class and Merit in the American High School* (New York: Longman's, 1978); James Rosenbaum, *Making Inequality* (New York: Wiley, 1976).
9. Philip Jackson, "Secondary Schooling for the Privileged Few," *Daedalus* 111 (Fall 1981), 125.
10. Goodlad, *A Place Called School*, ch. 5.
11. Thomas F. Green, "Excellence, Equity, and Equality: The Conflict of Ideals" (Syracuse University, School of Education, 1979), pp. 51–2.
12. Dewey, *Democracy and Education*, pp. 101–2.

Chapter 4

1. These themes are drawn from Stanley B. Elam (ed.), *A Decade of Gallup Polls of Attitudes Toward Education, 1969–1978* (Bloomington, Ill.: Phi

Delta Kappa, 1978), and the annual Gallup Polls published in *Phi Delta Kappan* through September 1984.

2. Stanley N. Wellborn, "Ahead: A Nation of Illiterates," *US News and World Report,* May 17, 1982, 53–7.

3. Patricia Albjerg Graham, "Literacy, A Case for Secondary Schools," *Daedalus* 110 (Summer 1981), 119.

4. John Passmore, *The Philosophy of Teaching* (Cambridge, Mass.: Harvard University Press, 1980); Jerome Bruner, *On Knowing* (Cambridge, Mass.: Belknap Press of Harvard University Press, 1979).

5. Joseph Featherstone, "An American Education," *Commonwealth School Newsletter* (1982), 5.

6. P. B. Medawar, *Advice to a Young Scientist* (New York: Harper Colophon Books, 1979), p. 93.

7. Passmore, *The Philosophy of Teaching,* pp. 145–65. We draw heavily on these pages in Passmore for our discussion of imaginative behavior.

8. Ibid., pp. 180–1.

9. Suzanne Langer, *Philosophy in a New Key* (Cambridge, Mass.: Harvard University Press, 1942), p. 276.

10. Julian Haes, "Conceptions of the Curriculum: Teachers and 'Truth'," *British Journal of Sociology of Education* 3, 1 (1982), 62–3; Philip A. Cusick, *The Egalitarian Ideal and the American High School* (New York: Longman's, 1983).

11. Quoted in Paul H. Hirst, "Liberal Education and the Nature of Knowledge," in Reginald D. Archeaubault (ed.), *Philosophical Analysis and Education* (New York: Humanities Press, 1965).

12. See especially John Dewey, *Art as Experience* (New York: Capricorn Books, 1958; originally 1934); also Elliot Eisner, *Cognition and Curriculum* (New York: Longman's, 1982); Nelson Goodman, *Languages of Art* (Indianapolis, Ind.: Hackett, 1975); *Coming to Our Senses,* The Arts, Education and Americans Panel (New York: McGraw-Hill, 1977).

13. Goodman, *Languages of Art,* p. 249; Bruner, *On Knowing,* p. 3.

14. Michael Polyani, *Personal Knowledge* (Chicago: University of Chicago Press, 1958), p. 15.

15. John Passmore, *Science and Its Critics* (New Brunswick, N.J.; Rutgers University Press, 1978), p. 75; see also pp. 69–100. See also Passmore, *Art, Science, and Imagination* (Sydney: Sydney University Press, 1975).

16. For a collection of essays on scientific literacy, see *Daedalus* 112 (Spring 1983).

17. National Science Board Commission on PreCollege Education, Mathematics, Science, and Technology, *Educating Americans for the 21st Century* (Washington, D.C.: National Science Board, 1983).

18. Lawrence Weschler, "Profile: Robert Irwin," *The New Yorker,* March 8, 1982, p. 80.

19. Bruner, *On Knowing,* p. 118.

20. Theodore R. Sizer, *Horace's Compromise: The Dilemmas of the Amer-*

ican High School (Boston: Houghton Mifflin, 1984), indicates some of these directions.

21. Sara Lawrence Lightfoot, "Portraits of Exemplary Secondary Schools: St. Paul's School," *Daedalus* 110 (Summer 1981), 105.

22. David Owen, *High School* (New York: Viking Press, 1981), p. 37.

23. See John Passmore, *Philosophy of Teaching* (Cambridge, Mass.: Harvard University Press, 1980), ch. 8.

24. Howard Gardner, *Frames of Mind: A Theory of Multiple Intelligences* (New York: Basic Books, 1983). See also Eisner, *Cognition and Curriculum.*

25. Thomas F. Green, "Weighing the Justice of Inequality," *Change* 12 (July/August 1980), 26–32.

Chapter 5

1. Leo Marx, *The Machine in the Garden: Technology and the Pastoral Ideal in America* (New York: Oxford University Press, 1964); Lewis Mumford, *Technics and Civilization* (New York: Harcourt, Brace and World, 1934).

2. Henry Adams, *The Education of Henry Adams* (Boston: Houghton Mifflin, 1918), ch. 25.

3. David L. Waltz, "Artificial Intelligence," *Scientific American* 247 (October 1982), 118–33.

4. For a discussion, see *Daedalus* 109 (Winter 1980) and *Daedalus* 111 (Fall 1982).

5. Henry Jay Backer, *Microcomputers in the Classroom – Dreams and Realities,* Report No. 319 (Baltimore: Johns Hopkins University, Center for the Social Organization of Schools). Many of the themes developed here parallel issues raised in Harold Howe II, "Computers – the New Kick in Schools: An Overview," Speech to the Institute on Computing in Schools, Harvard University Graduate School of Education, (Cambridge, Mass.: August 10, 1982).

6. Harold G. Sloan, "The Silicon Age and Education," *Phi Delta Kappan* 63 (January 1982), 306.

7. Charles Dickens, *Hard Times* (New York: Dutton, 1907), ch. 1.

8. Boris Pasternak, cited in Philip J. Davis and Reuben Hersh, *The Mathematical Experience* (Boston: Birkhauser, 1981).

9. Seymour Papert, *Mindstorms* (New York: Basic Books, 1980).

10. Papert, *Mindstorms,* presents an extensive discussion of Project Logo.

11. Dale La Frenz, "Corporate Viewpoints on Computers in Education," *Educational Technology* 22 (March 1982), 27.

12. Barbara Andrews and David Hakkan, "Educational Technology: A Theoretical Discussion," *College English* (September 1977), 81.

13. NEA unpublished survey, cited in *Education Week,* January 12, 1983, p. 1.

14. William Barrett, *The Illusion of Technique* (New York: Doubleday, 1978).

15. Maxine Greene, "Literacy For What?" *Phi Delta Kappan* 63 (January 1982), p. 328.

Chapter 6

1. From a Berkeley meeting with teachers during preparation of this book, May 9, 1981.

2. From a Chicago meeting with teachers during preparation of this book, June 3, 1981.

3. See Donna H. Kerr, "Teaching Competence and Teacher Education in the U.S.," *Teachers College Record* 84 (Spring 1983), 525–52, and the other articles in the same issue. See also Theodore R. Sizer, *Horace's Compromise: The Dilemma of the American High School* (Boston: Houghton Mifflin, 1984), pp. 9–22, 141–202.

4. Thomas Toch, "No Direction, No Accountability: Why the Inservice System Breaks Down," *Education Week*, October 6, 1982.

5. This section owes much to Jean V. Carew and Sara Lawrence Lightfoot, *Beyond Bias: Perspectives on Classrooms* (Cambridge, Mass.: Harvard University Press, 1979); Sara Lawrence Lightfoot, *The Good High School: Portraits of Character and Culture* (New York: Basic Books, 1983); Philip Jackson, *Life in Classrooms* (New York: Holt, Rinehart and Winston, 1968); Dan Lortie, *Schoolteacher* (Chicago: University of Chicago Press, 1975); Ernest Boyer, *High School* (New York: Harper & Row, 1983); Barbara Neufeld, "Making Passive Students Active," *Education Week*, November 10, 1982, p. 20.

6. Willard Waller, *The Sociology of Teaching* (New York: Wiley, 1932); Jackson, *Life*, p. 48.

7. Philip A. Cusick, *The Egalitarian Ideal and the American High School: Studies of Three Schools* (New York: Longman's, 1983), p. 94.

8. Lortie, *Schoolteacher*, pp. 168–73.

9. Ibid.

10. Ibid., pp. 117–29.

11. Ibid., p. 98.

12. Harold Howe II, "Improving Pedagogy," speech to chief state school officers of the United States, White Sulphur Springs, West Virginia, November 17, 1980.

13. For the RAND study, see Paul Berman and Milbrey McLaughlin, *Federal Programs Supporting Educational Change,*Vol. IV, *The Findings in Review,* R-1589/4-HES (Santa Monica, Calif.: Rand Corporation, April 1975); Milbrey McLaughlin and David March, "Staff Development and School Change," *Teachers College Record* 80 (September 1978). For a discussion of the effect of school culture on efforts at change, see Seymour Sarason, *The Culture of the School and the Problem of Change,* 2nd ed. (Boston: Allyn and Bacon, 1982).

14.   Harry F. Wolcott, *Teachers Versus Technocrats: An Educational Innovation in Anthropological Perspective* (Eugene, Ore.: Center for Educational Policy and Management, University of Oregon, 1977), p. 148.

15.   McLaughlin and March, "Staff Development," 74.

16.   Ibid., 73.

17.   Larry Cuban, "Teacher as Leader and Captive: Continuity and Change in American Classrooms, 1890–1980," ch. 6 (ERIC System: National Institute of Education, Grant No. NIE G-81-0024, 1982); Stewart C. Puckey and Marshall S. Smith, "Too Soon to Cheer? Synthesis of Research on Effective Schools," *Educational Leadership* 40 (December 1982), 64–9.

18.   John Passmore, *The Philosophy of Teaching* (Cambridge, Mass.: Harvard University Press, 1980), p. 24.

19.   Israel Scheffler, *Reason and Teaching* (London: Routledge & Kegan Paul, 1973), p. 67.

INDEX

ability grouping(s), 10–12
  and behavioral attributes, 12
  conditions surrounding, 10
  on different school levels, 12, 55
  and IQ, 10–11
  in junior high school, 12
  justifications for, 11
  in nineteenth century, 10
  in senior high school, 12
  see also tracking
academic rigor, 17–18
  turning away from, and shift in
    priorities, 32
accountability, teachers', 12–13, 97, 107–8
achievement, low, and low expecta-
    tions, 57
administrative efficiency, and ability
    grouping, 11
administrator(s)
  as "old boy," 13
  scrutiny of, 13
aesthetics, 74, 75
age grading, 7, 10
analytic skills, *see* skills, analytic
arts, 74, 75
attendance, school
  compulsory, 15
  daily, 7
  mass, 7
  variations in, 19
Ayres, Leonard, 7, 8

bargaining, classroom, 99–100
basic skills, *see* skills, basic

behavioral attributes, and ability group-
    ing, 12
Binet, Alfred, 8, 9
black schools, 5–6
brain, right and left hemispheric func-
    tions of, 72
Bruner, Jerome, 24, 34, 38, 41, 45, 66,
    74, 77
bureaucratization, 13

*Cardinal Principles of Secondary Educa-
    tion*, 16–17
caring, by teachers, 102
Catholics
  and parochial schools, 5
  and religious conflicts, 5
citizenship
  and democracy, 56–7, 60–1, 66
  education for, 4, 53, 56–7, 60–1
  and educational conversation, 73
  equality necessary for, 50, 51
  excellence necessary for, 51
  failure of, 61
  imaginative expression and critical
    thinking necessary for, 71
  and inequality, 61
  and schools as minimalist institu-
    tions, 66
  and scientific literacy, 75
class divisions
  and computer access, 85–6, 87
  and elementary schools, 11
  and occupational grouping in high
    school, 12
  and tracking, 55, 57, 60
class size, 118

133

Index

ethnicity
  and conflict, 5
  and learning capacities, 8
  and racism, 8
evaluative system, for teachers, 119
excellence, 4
  as challenge, 113–15
  and computers, 83
  and critical thinking, 71, 114–15
  definitions of, 113, 114, 115
  and economic payoffs, 53
  and fear of inequality, 50
  and imaginative expression, 71, 114–15
  and literacy, 64–72, 114–15
  as necessity for citizenship, 51, 61
  renewed call for, 49, 50
  tensions between equality and, 41, 45–6, 50, 115
expectations
  historical, 3–22
  low, and low achievement, 57
  and tracking, 55–7, 59
expression, imaginative, 61, 68–70, 71
  and basic skills, 65–6, 72, 114–15
  and computers, 94
  dimensions and forms of, 69
  and science, 75, 76
  teaching for, 69–70

facts, vs. knowledge and education, 87–8
fads, educational, 68, 116
family, economic needs of, 15
foreign language instruction, 43
freedmen's schools, 5–6

gender
  and computer use, 86–7
  and employment discrimination, 20, 21, 86
  and occupational groupings in high school, 12
  occupational stratification by, 20
  and tracking, 60
general program, and tracking, 59
genetics, and learning capacity, 8, 9–10

high school
  ability levels of individual classes in, 55
  courses of study in, and tracking, 53, 55
  enrollment in, increased, 19
  graduation requirements in, and science and mathematics, 76
  see also junior high school; schooling, extended; secondary education; senior high school
historical expectations, 3–22
historical perspective, 3–22, 111

illiteracy, functional, 64
imaginative expression, *see* expression, imaginative
immigrants
  racist assumptions about, 8
  see also ethnicity
individual differences, *see* differences, individual
inequality
  and computer use, 85–7
  economic, 51–4
  and tracking, 55–60
  and vocational education, 58–9
  see also equality
integrated schools, 5, 50
intelligence, and equality and excellence, 113
intelligence, flexible, and imaginative
  and critical thinking, 68
intelligence (IQ) tests, 8–10
  and tracking, 52
intelligences, multiple, 80, 113
  see also differences, individual
interests, differences in, 54, 57
IQ tests, *see* intelligence tests

junior high school
  ability levels of individual classes in, 55
  courses of study in, and tracking, 52, 55
  and differentiation of students, 12
  see also high school; secondary education

Index

knowing, and learning, 72–80
knowledge, objective vs. subjective, 72–3

Laggards in the Schools (Ayres), 7–8
leadership, educational, 120–1
learning
  attitudes toward, 66
  and brain hemispheres, 72
  commitment to, 101, 115
  compensatory, 32
  and computers, 94 (*see also* computers)
  content vs. process in, 72
  and educational conversation, 73–9, 109–10
  expansive, 65, 66–72, 77–8, 94
  hierarchical steps of, 66
  for its own sake, 122
  and knowing, 72–80
  to learn, 71, 72
  literacy as basis for, 65
  and making meaning, 80
  and objective vs. subjective knowledge, 72–3
  as process of growth, 71
  self-directed, 72
  scientific and aesthetic, integrating, 77
  to think, 71, 72
learning ability
  differences in, 51, 52, 54, 57 (*see also* differences, individual)
  and genetics, 8, 9–10
  and racism, 8, 9–10
learning environments, 119–20
literacy
  and analytic skills, 65
  and basic skills, 64, 65, 115–16
  as basis for learning, 65
  and citizenship, 4, 61
  computer, 83, 93
  definitions of, 65
  and excellence, 64–72, 114, 115–16
  scientific, 75–6
  and tracking, 56, 58–9
  views of, limiting, 64–5
  and vocational education, 58

Man: A Course of Study (MACOS), 33–42
  controversy over, 36, 38–40, 41–2, 44–5
  teachers' problems with, 35, 36, 40–1
  and values, 14, 38, 39, 40, 44
mathematics
  new, *see* School Mathematics Study Group (SMSG)
  numbers of students taking, 76
meaning, making, and learning, 80
memorization, learning by, 6–7
Mishler, Anita, 35, 37
morality, and origins of public education, 4, 5

National Education Association (NEA)
  Commission on the Reorganization of Secondary Education, 16–17
  Committee of Ten, 16
new English, 43
new mathematics, *see* School Mathematics Study Group (SMSG)
new science, 43
new social studies, see *Man: A Course of Study*

occupational categories, 9–10, 12, 20
Oliver, Douglas, 34

parents
  disadvantages of, as obstacles to children, 55
  intervention of, 12, 13, 15
  and *Man: A Course of Study,* 39, 40, 44
  problems of, with new mathematics, 31–2
  tracking resisted by, 11
  values of, 13, 14, 39
parochial schools, 5
pedagogical efficiency, and ability grouping, 11
performance, school, surveys of, 7–8
planning, collaborative, and improvements in teaching, 105, 106–8
political equality, education for, 50–1, 53

136

Index

politics, and origins of public education, 4
principals, 120–1
private schools, 112, 121
process vs. content, 72
professionalization, of public education, 14
Project Logo, 88–9
Protestantism, and origins of public education, 4
Protestants, and religious conflict, 5
public support, for public education, 121

race
  and conflict, 5–6
  and occupational groupings in high school, 12
  segregation by, in elementary school, 12
  and tracking, 55, 57, 60
racism, and learning ability, 8, 9–10
reform, curriculum
  failure of, 32–3
  of 1950s and 1960s, 23–46
  university scholars' involvement in, 23–4, 26, 33, 43–4
  see also *Man: A Course of Study;* School Mathematics Study Group
reform, school, 111–22
  outside origins of, 104–5
  school as best unit of, 105–6
  and teachers, 104–6
religion, and origins of public education, 4–5
religious values
  and *Man: A Course of Study,* 14, 36, 40
  tensions over, 14
repeaters, 7, 8
residential segregation, and tracking, 55
rural areas, and economic needs of family, 15

salaries, teachers', 96, 117
school(s)
  age-graded, 10
  criticisms of, continuing, 111–13

custodial function of, 71–2
educative power of, enhancing, 121–2
guiding principles needed by, 116
identity of, necessity for, 116
individual, as best unit for reform, 105–6
as minimalist institutions, 66
and private vs. public interests, 112
public support needed for, 121
size of, 119–20
see also specific types
school districts, and access to computers, 85–6, 87
School Mathematics Study Group (SMSG), 24–33
  computational skills, emphasis on, 27, 30, 44
  concepts, emphasis on, 27, 30, 44
  controversy over, 30–3, 44
  failure of, 32–3
  parents' problems with, 31–2
  teachers' attitudes toward, 30–1, 33
  and textbooks, 28–9, 30, 31, 33
schooling, extended
  economic benefits of, 15, 18–21, 51–4
  and learning ability, 12
  and occupational categories, 9–10, 12
  and vocational education, 20
science
  new, 43
  number of students taking, 76
  as part of educational conversation, 76–7
  teaching of, 76
scientific literacy, 75–6
scientific thinking, 75
secondary education
  and academic rigor, 17–18
  and comprehensive curriculum, 16–18
  see also high school; junior high school; senior high school
segregation, *see* class divisions; gender; race; residential segregation
senior high school
  and grouping by occupational categories, 9–10, 12
  see also high school; secondary education

137

Index